LIGHT FROM A DARK NIGHT

Anne M. Grove

Copyright © 2017 Anne Grove

All rights reserved. Published by Letter of Light

www.letteroflight.com

"Scripture quotations taken from the Amplified® Bible (AMP),
Copyright © 2015 by The Lockman Foundation
Used by permission. www.Lockman.org"

"Scripture quotations taken from the Amplified® Bible (AMPC),
Copyright © 1954, 1958, 1962, 1964, 1965, 1987 by The Lockman Foundation
Used by permission. www.Lockman.org"

Unless otherwise indicated, all Scripture quotations are taken from *THE MESSAGE*, copyright © 1993, 1994, 1995, 1996, 2000, 2001, 2002 by Eugene H. Peterson. Used by permission of NavPress. All rights reserved. Represented by Tyndale House Publishers, Inc.

Strong's Exhaustive Concordance of the Bible Updated and Expanded Edition 2007 Hendrickson Publishers, Inc.

Cover photo credit: Izf/Shutterstock

ISBN: 0692476393

ISBN-13: 978-0692476390

DEDICATION

With love, I dedicate this book:

To my parents- for a lifetime of love and for giving me the belief I could do anything.

To Rob, Gabrielle and Bella- Every day is an adventure! I love you all so much.

To Margie and Charlie – for your love and support.

To Carol- for friendship, prayers, and encouragement through the process of writing this book.

Special Thanks

To Jesus Christ- the true love of my life

LIGHT FROM A DARK NIGHT

Contents

DEDICATION	5
PREFACE	9
1 THE TEST OF ENDURANCE	13
2 THE SIGHTS OF BEIJING, CHINA	25
3 GOTCHA DAY	35
4 PLEASE DON'T EAT THE CRAB	47
5 BATTLE FOR YOUR CALLING	57
6 BATTLE FOR YOUR DREAM	79
7 BATTLE FOR YOUR STRENGTH IN CHRIST	103
8 ALONE IN CHINA	121
9 MOVING FORWARD	125
10 HELPLESS NOT HOPELESS	135

11 THE TEST OF SEPARATION	**145**
12 HEAVEN OPENS UP	**175**
13 SEEING INTO HEAVEN	**191**
14 FROM FLESH TO SPIRIT	**207**
15 ACCEPTING CHRIST AS REVEALED	**229**
16 THE POWER OF WORDS AND THOUGHTS	**235**
17 BECOME A VESSEL TO RULE	**267**
18 POSITIONED	**289**
ABOUT THE AUTHOR	**301**

PREFACE

I'm so glad you've chosen to read Light from a Dark Night. In this book I'll share my travel experience in China while adopting our daughter Bella. During those two weeks I went through several spiritual battles which culminated in the greatest test of faith I've ever experienced. I believe these battles and tests aren't exclusive to myself or someone adopting a child but carry meaning for all who aspire to fulfill God's plan for their life.

I never had any intentions of sharing my story until I came across this verse in the Bible:

- ❖ "Blessed [gratefully praised and adored] be the God and Father of our Lord Jesus Christ, the Father of mercies and the God of all comfort, [4] who comforts *and* encourages us in every trouble <u>so that we will be able to comfort *and* encourage those who are in any kind of trouble, with the comfort with which we ourselves are comforted by God.</u>"[i]

I started to think how reassuring it is to read a book and nod my head and say, "Yes, someone understands me and what I'm going through!" Many times the inspired voice of the author breathed new life into me and was the fuel which kept my faith alive and moving forward. In those moments I felt comforted knowing I was led by Holy Spirit to a particular author for a purpose. I hope you feel this way too and connect with my trials of being called, fulfilling a dream and being tested in the area of strength and authority in Christ. We do have different lives but one Lord who is shaping us through spiritual tests of various kinds so we come through the fire as pure gold.

I have enjoyed writing more than I ever thought possible. I've benefitted from sharing my experience and I've had reason to pray, study and contemplate spiritual testing as it relates to our faith today. At the end of it all I've concluded we should desire God to search our hearts on a regular basis and place our faith under fire. It's the only way we'll ever know the strength and depth to which we hold and reflect the image of Christ.

As the Body of Christ, let's do everything we can to encourage and inspire each other to win our faith battles. Together let's hold strong to what we have in Christ and then accelerate into the works God has prepared us in advance to do.[ii]

Anne Grove

Founder Letter of Light Ministries

LIGHT FROM A DARK NIGHT

1 The Test of Endurance

Since we've been back from China to adopt our daughter a while now[iii], I still cannot shake the feeling it's important for me to share my experience with you. I have thought of the trip often and as hard as it was I've come to the conclusion I can be thankful for the experience in several ways.

First I am thankful for our little Bella who was eleven months old at the time. Meeting her was everything I'd hoped it would be. And now seeing how our family is blending makes it worth all the pain associated with the adoption process.

Second I am thankful for the experience of being out of the United States for a short time. I gained a deep sense of appreciation for America while I was away.

Lastly, and most importantly, I am grateful for the spiritual battles I fought while there. Without them I would not know the authority which is mine and yours through Christ Jesus. This is the reason I'm writing you today because we fortify each other's faith when we share our experiences.

You are not alone in your walk of faith. All over the world there are others facing the same types of trials and battles of the soul. It's important to keep in mind God is at work even in the midst of trials, testing and temptations.

We should expect to be tested through various trials. None of them should disturb us to the point of giving up on our faith but should lead us to a closer relationship with Christ[iv]. Trials can be one method God uses to test our hearts expecting them to be approved.[v] He anticipates we will come through with flying colors and with a stronger faith than we had before. God has faith in our faith!

The spiritual battles I faced in China were intense and tumbled one right after another increasing in strength. The enemy designed a plan making our situation seem dark and bleak with no way out. I felt an intense fear for my life and the pressure was so great upon my soul I really thought I might die and never make it home. For this reason, I will always remember this experience as my "dark night of the soul".

My faith was put to the test by our unseen enemy in several key areas. I believe these key spiritual battles are not unique to me. At some point all of us need to become humble placing our strength on the ground to pick up the strength of Christ. In so doing we prove ourselves worthy of God's trust[vi] and we will complete the works He has chosen for us to walk in.

Don't worry if you are not going through an adoption or travelling out of the country. Jesus talked to us using earthly examples which illustrated heavenly principles. I'm writing about the field of my battle to highlight and bring to light yours - so you can take the spiritual truths I'm giving and apply them to your life.

Trust me, each and every believer will face a dark night in their soul. My writing isn't meant to keep you from your time of testing because we all need weaknesses exposed in order to sharpen strengths. Instead, this book will shed light on what kind of battles you may face as you grow in your walk of faith and increase your understanding of Christ.[vii]

Before I get to my dark night of the soul I want to fill you in on a little backstory of our adoption journey. We began our paperwork in February 2011 and were set to adopt a child from India when some regulations were updated regarding the ages of prospective parents and child. We were in the early phases of the process and decided to change our adoption country to Bulgaria. Our papers were officially filed in Bulgaria December 2011. After eleven months of paperwork, classes, and fingerprinting we had high hopes our dream of a little girl would be answered soon. But we heard from our adoption agency very little over the next year.

During this time of silence my husband and I were frustrated with the process. There were additional requests for more paperwork and money flowed out consistently for various things. Our friends and family asked us how the adoption was going and it was hard to keep saying we had no new information. With time passing by we felt like it was never going to happen and I was ready to give up. But keeping us going was our desire for another child, the money already invested, and a calling from God to adopt an orphan.

One day in November of 2012 almost a year after we'd filed in Bulgaria Amy (not her real name), our adoption consultant called to give a brief update. She had been checking on our status in Bulgaria and from her update I knew we were looking at several more years before we'd bring a little girl home.

She apologized for the lack of communication but said Bulgaria was not very easy to work with. The adoption agencies did not have any access to their list of waiting children (unlike other countries) to try and make matches for their clients. It was all based on a number system. When your number came up they matched you with whatever child was available no matter if the child fit your profile or not. Plus she said any waiting child in Bulgaria must be turned down three times by native citizens before they could be put up for international adoption.

This information did explain why we hadn't heard anything over the last year but it would have been nice to know it up front. There was simply nothing going to happen until our number came up. I was very upset and told her I was ready to give up. I was torn between the desire to have another child and with the facts of life. I was getting older and wasn't sure I'd want to go back to the diaper phase if we'd have to wait a few more years.

She listened to all my frustrations and said one possibility would be to switch countries and she suggested China. Amy said she was sure if we got going with the paperwork we would either be traveling to China or home with our child this same time next year. As she was talking something inside me knew this was the right move for us but I would have to talk to my husband first.

That night my husband and I talked over making the switch to China. Switching countries was easy to do in the beginning but since we were already registered in Bulgaria our decision would be more complex. We would lose a large sum of money already sent to Bulgaria and we'd have to do much of our paperwork over. But we both sensed it was right and felt compelled to act quickly.

Later we would find out all of this took place right about the time Bella was being born. Amy's words did became a reality as we travelled to China exactly one year later in November 2013.

Sometimes it's important to be flexible and willing to change if internally we "know in our knower" it's the right thing to do. We do our best when answering God's call and begin to follow the path we feel is right at the moment. But there are times when the time has just come when we have to do something to keep moving in step with the call even if it means making a change.

If we had not switched to China and worked quickly to make all the necessary changes I am most certain we would not have been in the right place and time for Bella. Our referral for Bella came one month after our papers were officially filed in

China. Amy called us late one night and set up a conference call as Rob was out of town for work.

We listened to Amy talk about this special little girl who needed a forever home. I took one look at her and was in love. Amy wanted us to think about it overnight but Rob and I both knew she was ours. He said, "God opened up a door for us and we'd better walk through it."

That began the longest six months of my life. We had a flow of paperwork between us and China and felt a constant desire to see a picture or hear something about her. But communication was rare as she was considered matched and the focus of the orphanage was on getting others adopted. We did get some pictures in August and they would have to hold us until we saw her in November.

We received word of our travel and had ten days to prepare for the trip. I felt like we were in a pressure cooker trying to get our visas on time, paperwork complete, pack and tie up loose ends.

My emotions went up and down and I felt like a basket case. I was thrilled just thinking about holding Bella yet was upset about leaving our seven year old daughter for two weeks. I was excited about the trip but was afraid of the unknowns travelling to another country. I called the adoption agency who said all of my feelings were completely normal and they helped by walking me through the trip a little bit.

On the spiritual side I was deeply grateful to God who answered our prayer for a baby. From the beginning we wanted a baby knowing the least amount of time in an orphanage would be for the best. We were told we'd never get a child under eighteen months old from Bulgaria and would have had to be open to a much older child. Making the change to China and entering their special needs program allowed us not only to get a child faster but younger. Somehow God made a way and gave us the desire of our hearts.

With all this to be thankful for I should have been jumping up and down for joy but for some reason I was almost depressed.

I thought it was just a let down from having to endure for so long in faith and prayer. I was tired from the long fight and wanted to go to China, get Bella, "and live happily ever after".

It's possible the heaviness I felt was a warning from the Holy Spirit to be on guard because despite what I wanted there would be reason for me to keep up my shield of faith. However this is the wisdom of hindsight. I didn't even entertain the idea then because I assumed my battle of faith was already won.

We'd made it through all sorts of road blocks, setbacks, and mental pressures. Certainly we endured the process. Now I realize endurance comes as a qualifier for Spiritual advancement and blessing. When your desired blessing finally does come you too may find enduring through the process was really the beginning and not the end of it all.

The longer your time of endurance the greater the impact on your life. You (and obviously me) need all the time we can get to prepare to hold the weight of what God wants us to have. If our calling was unimportant or easy then anyone would be able to do it. Instead, the seed of faith we have needs to be cared for and nourished over time. Then when our faith seed is ready to sprout up the root system needed to sustain it will be strong and perfect. Our character will have matured creating an unwavering hope in our eternal life able to withstand all the wind and storms bound to come our way.[viii]

Stay focused on the dream God has placed deep inside you knowing endurance will qualify you to carry it across the finish line. God is faithful.

LIGHT FROM A DARK NIGHT

2 The Sights of Beijing, China

On Wednesday morning November 7th our travel to China was officially underway. The flight was delayed from Chicago to Beijing but it didn't matter because we'd met up with three of the five families we were traveling with. It was nice to have time to get to know them and hear some of their journey up to this point.

Finally, it was time to board the plane. Just about midway down the hallway to enter the plane we were surprised to find one of the couples in our group had been stopped. They were being questioned by a female TSA agent. Another female agent was trying to restrain a large dog which was going crazy and barking loudly. We stopped to see if they were okay but the TSA agent with the dog told us to get moving and we quickly moved forward onto the plane.

Once inside the plane we stood at our seats straining to see if our new friends would make it through on time. They did and came to our seats to tell us the dog was specially trained to sniff out money. The agent questioned them on whether they'd declared the large amount of money they were carrying because if not it could be seized at the other side of our flight.

This created a crisis of sorts because we were all carrying large amounts of cash to finalize our adoptions. This is standard procedure for China adoptions and maybe other countries as well who require cash in specific denominations. We were told it wasn't necessary to declare it by our adoption agency since each person is allowed to carry a certain amount of cash into another country.

We quickly discussed our options: declare the money or live with the threat it could be confiscated on the other side. My husband decided we should declare it and ran down the aisle thinking he could get out to declare ours with the TSA agents. But the plane had already been loaded and was ready to go. We spent the rest of the flight concerned our money would be seized upon entry to China and our dreams to adopt would come to a terrible end.

The flight was 14 hours long and with five hours left to go I was cold and my legs started to cramp. I felt like I couldn't bear to sit any longer. We made casual friends with the lady seated in front of us and as we talked the time started to pass away. She was born in Hong Kong but is an Australian citizen and said she was a Christian. She was nice and a frequent traveler into China so we told her our dilemma over declaring our adoption money. She understood but told us not to worry. She said we would be ushered to walk right through customs without any problems.

By now we were nearing Beijing, China. Window shades started to open and beautiful rocky, black mountains appeared. I could see The Great Wall of China as I looked down. We were handed entry and exit Visa forms to fill out just as we were about to land.

The inside of the airport was dimly lit. There was no music or shops. No one was talking above a murmur and the silence seemed eerie to me. We were tense waiting in the immigration line hoping all of our papers were correct. There was an armed military guard marching up and down the yellow line between us and the government workers. The gentleman in front of me dropped his hat and as I stooped down to pick it up Rob yanked me backwards. Without thinking I would have crossed the yellow line and who knows what would have happened.

Once through immigration we walked quickly to customs. We agreed to go through the "declare" line as a group. If they stopped one of us for having a large sum of money they would have to stop us all. But true to the words of our friend on the plane we were told to keep moving and none of us were stopped. We all breathed a sigh of relief. Our guide was on the other side waiting for us and we boarded a private bus which took us to our hotel.

Our hotel was beautiful inside and it looked just like any other American hotel we'd stayed at. We didn't sleep well as the time difference from home was 13 hours. We woke up at 2 a.m. which would become the norm until we were accustomed to the time difference.

Our first morning in Beijing was bright and sunny and I will remember it as one of the highlights of my life. I never planned to travel outside of the United States and honestly if I had - I would never have picked China. But we were in Beijing traveling by bus to The Great Wall of China and I knew I was on the trip of a lifetime.

We arrived at The Great Wall of China and could see two sides of it from where we stood. Our guide suggested we take the "easy" climb which would take about an hour. That was fine with us as the other side was a four hour climb and it was much higher and steeper.

Our guide said it was very unusual for the day to be so clear which enabled us to see for miles. November is not the in season for tourists. We were alone for our climb with the exception of a few Chinese nationals. The steps were made of various sizes of stone and were so steep in parts I couldn't look up or down. I stopped at one point because I became paralyzed by fear of the heights. However I kept going and held up my hands in victory when I reached the top.

The views all around were breathtaking. As I walked along the stone structure I thought of the people who built it. How they must have struggled yet added detailed design to some of the stones. The climb down was just as steep in parts and I brought up the rear.

At the bottom of the steps was a tree with no leaves but the branches were covered with dangling red ribbons. The ribbons contained prayers written and hung by those who stopped at the nearby temple. They believe as the wind rustles the ribbons their prayers would be heard over and over. We walked by some souvenir tents and were ready to head back to the hotel.

Our second day in Beijing was packed seeing the sights. We went to Tiananmen Square, The Forbidden City, Olympic Park, Jade and Silk factories. It was a dismal looking day and the air quality is every bit as bad as you may have heard. Many wore masks.

I was totally surprised that the highways looked just like our American roads including toll roads. The medians were lined with red roses in bloom and one type of tree flowered with pink blooms. There were lots of weeping willow trees, junipers and plum bushes. I did not see any semi-trucks in the city but lots of bicyclists hauling material on carts.

The city itself is huge with crowds of people everywhere you looked. Beijing is home to twenty million people and there just aren't any spots which seemed private. Busses were jammed full of people and they do not stop for pedestrians!

I could not define the city as having a clear architectural style as new construction is built right next to seeming ruins. In reference to the buildings our guide kept saying "everything is new here" but nothing looked new because of the soot. The closer we got to Tiananmen Square we saw a very old section where the homes looked like shacks. However the property value is in the millions because of where they are located.

Tiananmen Square was our first stop and it was jam packed with thousands of tourists similar to what you'd see in

Washington D.C. The tourists were mostly from China and we saw a few people from other European countries. The Square is a large concrete square with several monuments and buildings of importance on each side. That day security was very high. There had been a terrorist car bombing the week before so we went through several military check points. The guards did not seem interested in Americans and passed us through without much a second look. It still felt scary though as we were very aware we were not in America.

While waiting in line to enter the Forbidden City three activist events took place right in front of us. All three activists were turned in by their own country men, captured by military and hauled away in a military truck. Our group huddled together as we were imagining the fate of those captured. A few of us stated we wanted to leave and go back to our hotel. We did not feel safe and didn't want any incident to disrupt our adoptions. However, our guide had us press on and we did enjoy seeing the artistry of the Forbidden City.

For lunch, our guide took us to a restaurant that served Peking duck. Most restaurants serve family style loading up food on a spinning disk in the center of the table. Everything looked and smelled good but I am not an adventurous eater. I ate rice with seasoned sugar snap peas. It tasted excellent and everyone else raved about the other dishes that were served.

After a couple of days in Beijing, I was missing our daughter Gabrielle badly. We were keeping in touch via video chats but it's not the same as being with her in person. I was also feeling weak from not eating well. Breakfast was my best meal of the day as the hotel catered to American's on the buffet. There was always bacon and pastries. I struggled to eat anything but rice or noodles for the other meals. One night we ventured out and found a Pizza Hut. Our waiter knew no English but kept a smile on his face the whole time and did a great job.

The water in China is not drinkable and we constantly had to bear that in mind when eating out. Eating raw food like lettuce was out because it may have been washed with the water. We had to buy bottled water or boil tap water in our rooms even to brush our teeth.

Lastly, the toilet situation was a real problem for me and others in our group. Our hotel was perfectly Americanized inside the room but outside it was difficult and sometimes not possible to find an American style toilet with toilet paper. We carried tissues with us at all times just in case. We were getting through it together and our group became very close in a short amount of time.

After several days in Beijing it was time for the second leg of our journey and we flew to Nanjing. I was anxious to keep the trip moving forward. We had a little girl waiting for us and while the sightseeing was nice we were focused on our reason for being in China.

3 Gotcha Day

We flew from Beijing to Nanjing, China with our guide and four other couples. We were pleasantly surprised by the airline and staff. The flight attendants all dressed to perfection and we were served full meals even though our flight was very short.

As we lowered altitude I could see the dark mountains had given way to lots of green space. I saw farmland and trees. There were smaller ponds scattered about surrounded by clusters of three story dwelling units.

The interior of the airport was modern with lots of shops. It had a decidedly different atmosphere than what we'd experienced at the Beijing Airport. Upon stepping outside we all paused and took note the air smelled clean. We took deep breaths of the fresh air as we walked to our van. Nanjing was further south and warmer than Beijing kind of like North Carolina would be to New York. I saw one lone American car in the parking lot and it was a Jeep. All of the cars were either black, white or silver. The only cars of any other colors were taxis.

Nanjing is a city of eight million people. Many areas in China have bamboo or dirt roads but we were lucky to be in large cities where the roads were paved just like they are in America. As we were riding to the hotel I sensed this was a people who cared about beauty. Landscaping projects were in full swing along the roadside and there was trailing greenery in flower boxes on major highway interchanges to hide the concrete.

It was Sunday and there were people working along the roadside using shovels not bulldozers to move masses of dirt. I thought it was quite an accomplishment as the workers (including many women) looked quite old. I saw willow trees, locust trees and what looked like one maple tree. The foliage was still green with leaves still on the trees and marigolds along the road were in late bloom.

We drove by an Ikea store, American automotive plants and manufacturing plants such as Kimberly Clark. Like Beijing, the architectural style was hard to pinpoint because the new was built right next to the old. There was an explosion of twenty story high rises next to very old housing units. There were no neighborhoods with single family houses. Everything was being built to accommodate a large amount of people.

Judging from the older cars on the road I thought this area must be less well off financially than Beijing where every car looked brand new. The fresh air we'd had at the airport disappeared as we entered the city. The closer we got to our hotel the more people I saw and the more chaotic the streets and sidewalks became.

Our hotel was very busy as a Chinese calligraphy convention was winding down. Our room was large but the air conditioning did not work. We were on the twelfth floor and it was warm. We opened a window and even being up so high the smell of the air was so bad it burned the inside of our noses.

That night we went out into the local market which was like something straight out of a movie. There were live animals for sale along with insects on a stick. This area invented the particular way of cooking Peking duck and dried ducks hung everywhere. It was so crowded in the streets I clung to Rob most of the night and was determined to stick close to our guide. Unlike Beijing, there were no other people of non-Asian descent except for our group. One woman in a side shop beamed brightly as she said "hi" to Rob. This was the only English she knew and was so happy to be able to use it.

Our hotel was connected to a very large three story mall which was as modern as any in the States. We had lots of food options including Subway and Papa John's Pizza. We debated on which to go to and opted for the pizza. We could not risk eating fresh lettuce or vegetables washed with the Chinese water. None of us wanted to get sick on the eve of meeting our new children. The pizza tasted so good and it was the first satisfying meal I'd had since eating at Pizza Hut in Beijing.

The outside air had been cold and damp as we'd walked through the market and I came in from the night with a sore throat and my ears hurt. I decided to start on an antibiotic I brought for emergency use right away. We went to bed knowing the next day would be life changing.

Finally, the day we'd been dreaming about arrived: it was "Gotcha Day"! It was also my birthday and after all the setbacks and delays in our adoption process how could anyone but God orchestrate such a birthday gift? When we were busy doing paperwork and enduring the agony of waiting for our child there were times when all I could see were the setbacks. Yet we kept believing God said we should adopt a child even when we didn't see how it was ever going to happen. Today we would receive the fruit of our faith.

Maybe you are in the same boat as I was and only seeing the setbacks in your life. I want to encourage you to keep believing in what God called and enabled you to do. He can make every set back and delay work for your good so you arrive to your moment right on time.

We boarded our bus about mid-morning and our ride to the Children's services building was tense. Everyone was nervous, anxious and filled with a broad range of emotions. We had no idea what to expect or how our child would react to us.

Once there we waited for the children who were late. We were told what direction they'd be coming from and all of us focused our eyes and camera's on those windows. Suddenly we saw some adults with children in their arms and in strollers. All of our cameras started going off just like Paparazzi.

The children were brought in and at first we had no idea which one was Bella. We hadn't seen a picture of her in 4 months at which time she had a shaved head. With hair, and being older she didn't look anything like I'd expected. Finally, I located her being held by the orphanage director.

She was more beautiful than I'd imagined and was quiet and staring blankly. She had no idea what was about to happen.

Bella was placed in my arms first. I held this little beauty I'd fallen in love with at first sight just six months ago. I had longed to hold her in my arms and show her how much I loved her. She stared at me with her big black eyes never looking around. Bella didn't cry but I did. How could I not? She had just given me the moment I'd been dreaming of. I passed her over to Rob and she looked at him then rested her head on his shoulder. We were so happy. In this state we were introduced to the orphanage director who handed us a brown bag of medicine for eczema. We thanked her but didn't think to ask her any questions about it.

As we were waiting for some documents to be completed by each family we marveled at how tiny and quiet Bella was. We finished paperwork, pictures and then boarded our bus which would take us back to the hotel. Bella did well during the bus ride and wanted to touch everything. The Chinese do not use car seats so I held her in my arms.

Everyone told us we'd want to bathe her right away giving her "our smell" so we did. She was so tiny almost like a six month old. We did the best we could in the bathroom sink. She had bumps and scabs all over her body and bleeding scabs on her scalp. The palms of her hands were really bad looking; she had scratched herself to the point of gauging out skin. Our hearts were breaking for her having to endure obvious itching and pain. We wished we could have been there for her sooner.

We knew Bella had dermatology issues but honestly seeing them in person was more than we could handle in this moment. On some level we felt like we'd not been told all we should have. Had we seen and been told everything would that have changed our mind about adopting Bella? Absolutely not, but it would have been nice to be prepared mentally and have proper medicine.

Now we wondered about the brown bag of medicine for eczema which had come with Q-tips and gloves. It was calamine lotion which I'd used at home for itchy insect bites and wondered why we'd been given the gloves. We had so many emotions and questions swirling around in our heads but there was not enough time to dwell on those because we were full swing into taking care of our new daughter.

We were focused on attachment and bonding which included meeting all of her needs quickly. We held her almost all of the time. Play time happened on the king size bed with one toy at a time. She could not sit up on her own without falling forward. Rob knew she needed muscle strength in her neck and started helping her up in such a way to do that. He was determined she learn to crawl and began playing with her encouraging movement.

Bella was really quiet probably taking all of her new surroundings and attention in. She only cried when her diaper was wet. She stared at us with thankfulness when we rubbed lotion onto her hands and especially seemed to like her hair being washed. She smiled and had a look of incredible wonder each time we fed her on her very own schedule.

Rob let me stay in the room with Bella while he went to the grocery store on the basement level of the mall. We needed more bottled water for formula and ourselves. It was easier than boiling water all the time. He bought several jars of baby food, rice cereal and lotions that might help her skin. We began putting Vaseline into the palms of her hands hoping to heal them.

The song which came to my mind while rocking Bella to sleep for the very first time was, "Jesus loves you this I know, for the Bible tells me so…" As I sang, she fell asleep and we made a makeshift bed for her between us. The hotel had run out of cribs and this would have to do. We didn't sleep much this first night with Bella. We kept making sure she was sleeping alright between us and we stared at this new child of ours. We loved her so much and could not wait to get her home.

LIGHT FROM A DARK NIGHT

LIGHT FROM A DARK NIGHT

4 Please Don't Eat the Crab

I woke up at 2 a.m. early Tuesday morning but laid in bed. I had all sorts of thoughts about Bella's skin going through my mind. I was afraid it was scabies and had been itching all over since the previous day. But how could it be scabies? She had come from the best orphanage. It was supposed to be impeccably clean and the children very well taken care of. None of the other children had the bumps like Bella and it just didn't make sense. We were hopeful for some answers later as we'd sent pictures through email of her rash to our doctor at home.

At 5 a.m. I did a video call with Gabrielle catching her just before dinner. I spoke with Rob's mom who said Gabrielle's mysterious rash (which she had just before we left for China) had become worse and she needed to go back to the doctor. I tried to talk to Gabrielle and hung up with her frustrated. I knew something was wrong and just couldn't pull it out of her. I sent a quick message to Rob's sister asking if she knew of anything upsetting Gabrielle.

She wrote back and said at school two of Gabrielle's classmates made fun of her on the playground knowing she was missing her parents. Reading this, my heart broke and I was very upset. I was too far away and could not comfort my daughter which weighed on me heavily. I was angry at the boys and just couldn't believe they could be so heartless.

After a while of being angry I decided the only way for me to get through the day was to forgive the boys and send email notes to my friends asking them to join me in prayer for Gabrielle. I knew I couldn't handle this alone and needed support. My deepest wish was for time to pass by faster so I could get home to see Gabrielle.

Bella woke up and was eating and drinking well. So well she gave me a diaper blowout which required me to send out all my clothes for cleaning! Late morning we returned to the Children's welfare center for notarization of paperwork needed for our daughter's Chinese passport. I had to use the restroom and gagged to the point of almost vomiting at their conditions. Another mom waited for me knowing I was having a hard time.

We left there and went back to the hotel. We needed to pack because the next morning we were checking out of our hotel for a day and travelling by train to visit the girls' orphanage. We'd be staying overnight and then travelling back to Nanjing. We were all stressed out about this trip. First, we were tired and second we thought it would be more trauma on the children to go back to the place they were never supposed to go back to.

Upon returning to the hotel we had several email messages from home. My sister in law sent our photos of Bella's skin to two doctors who both said Bella had scabies. One doctor was our pediatrician who said not to worry, "With medicine it would clear up within a couple days of our return home". However, we were distraught. Scabies is passed skin to skin and we were both itching like crazy. I had been searching online and knew we should be handling our clothing and bedding in a special way. But being in a hotel this was just not possible.

With over a week left in China we felt it was too long to wait for medicine for the scabies. We called our guide and wondered what we should do. He came right to our room with one of the other parents who was an E.R. doctor. The doctor looked at Bella closely and felt it was not scabies but eczema. He told us to apply hydrocortisone cream to the scabs and in time the bumps on her skin would all clear up. Our guide agreed to get us the hydrocortisone and said there would be a doctor at the orphanage who could look at Bella the next day.

We chose to believe the E.R. doctor because he was on site and could look at Bella closely. It had been hard for us to touch Bella's skin because we were afraid of getting scabies. But as her mother I had to touch her. Not only did I have to but I wanted to touch her to bond and make a strong connection.

After they left our hotel room I broke down. I poured out my heart to Rob. I wasn't feeling good and was hungry. The snacks I'd packed from the U.S. were gone. I was depressed and wanted to see Gabrielle to comfort her. I missed her more than I ever thought possible. I still felt Bella needed to get to a doctor and tomorrow wasn't soon enough. Life in China was hard with boiling the water in our rooms and everything else. We had nine days left in the trip and it seemed like forever.

Even though the morning had been draining we had many bright moments with Bella. She was bonding to us quite well. She missed Rob when he was at the grocery store and lit up when he returned. I was melting as she kissed me and she would cry if I walked out of her sight. She was smiling a lot and that was a big deal. Smiles were not the first reaction from any of the girls. Most of them were quiet taking in their new found love, attention and food as if it were a dream that might end.

Our group ate dinner together opting for the hotel buffet. We all had a lot of packing left to do. I had spaghetti marinara and Rob had spaghetti with meat sauce. The hotel staff brought each one of us a complimentary cooked crab (it was whole and on a plate). We all declined the crab except Rob. He was intrigued by it and asked the waiter how he would open and eat it.

After the waiter explained how to cut open the crab he stood there expecting Rob to follow his directions. I knew Rob felt obligated to eat a little but I told him not to as our travel papers specifically said don't eat seafood. But he ate anyway not wanting to hurt the feelings of the hotel staff who was kind to us.

We left for our room after eating and I tried to clean up the bombshell in our room. We had to check out in the morning before leaving for the orphanage so everything had to be packed tonight. Again, we both had mixed emotions. We wanted to see where Bella had been staying and the spot where she had been abandoned mostly so we could tell her about it one day. We also wanted her to be seen by a doctor.

But we didn't look forward to the travel or to Bella possibly getting reattached to her caregivers.

Within a few minutes of getting back to the room Rob was sick. He was violently sick which made us think it was food poisoning. He thought it was the spaghetti but others who had eaten the same thing weren't sick. I knew though, it was the crab!

I couldn't muster up an "I told you so" because he was feeling so bad. All he could do was sit in the bathroom on the floor. I did whatever I could for him. He had been my rock so far and now my rock was down. Suddenly I had to take care of him, Bella and pack for the trip. I called our guide and told him how sick Rob was. I wasn't sure if we could travel in the morning. He offered to take Rob to a hospital but Rob wanted to stay in the room.

We knew a lot was at stake including train tickets and hotel reservations. I'm not sure I could convey how bleak and dark things seemed then. I felt alone and didn't know what to do. I felt pressured to go on the trip and leave Rob behind.

After rocking Bella to sleep, I did a video chat with my sister in law who was my greatest support during this trip. It was dark in our room as I talked to her and we felt like spies communicating about a secret mission. I told her I was scared for Rob because he was so sick. And, I was scared for me. All the snacks I'd brought from home were gone and I didn't know what to eat. She offered to ship some food to our hotel but I thought it would get confiscated and never get to us in time.

Also, Rob had been going to the grocery store getting water and all the miscellaneous things we needed. I didn't think I could find the way by myself because the mall was laid out in circles. It all looked the same to me. Nor was I willing to try it alone with Bella and risk getting lost. I said goodnight to her ending the video chat and lay down on the bed.

About 11 a.m. I sent an email message to two families in our group to see if either one had some anti-nausea medicine. One family did and brought it to our room. Rob took the medicine and eventually he fell asleep. However sleep did not come to me as this was the night of my great spiritual battles. My dark night of the soul was here and it felt like I was battling for my very life.

LIGHT FROM A DARK NIGHT

5 Battle for Your Calling

Just after Rob fell asleep from the anti-nausea medicine I lay awake crying as quietly as I could. I was intensely battling to make a decision of whether to stay in Nanjing with Rob who was sick or leave him and go by train on an overnight trip with the rest of our group to Bella's orphanage where she could be seen by a doctor.

As I was thinking about what to do I became aware of a strong presence of fear. My body prickled all over and I felt paralyzed by fear while trying to determine where it was coming from. Since no one else but us was in the room I concluded it was a very dangerous spirit trying to overpower my senses to make me believe my life was at risk. I tried to ignore my feelings of fear by thinking about our daughter Gabrielle.

I spoke to her through a video call before going to bed and was having a hard time talking to her. I wanted to be upbeat but was missing her so much I started crying. I felt absolutely horrible for not being able to hug her and be there for her everyday life.

I was really worried about the rash on her leg. It had been there for a while and I didn't think much of it until a few days before leaving for China. The rash became bigger so I took her to our Pediatrician the day before we left. He didn't know what the rash was specifically but prescribed a cream and said to come back if it did not go away.

Yesterday, when I knew the cream had not helped I started looking up rashes on the internet while in the hotel room. The rash looked like pictures of Lyme disease. Since the rash appeared after a soccer game it was plausible the rash began with a tick bite. I regretted not taking Gabrielle to the doctor right away and was afraid I'd done something to hurt her for life.

All of a sudden as I was thinking along those lines I heard what sounded like screams being directed toward me, "You left your daughter- you call yourself a good mother? How could you leave her when she needs you?" These screams did not come from within me but were loud, screechy and furious sounding. A threatening, fiery dart from a satanic enemy had been sent my way.

In my heart I felt some truth to those accusations and questioned myself, "Yeah, how could I call myself a good mother? I didn't take care of Gabrielle and her rash like I should have. How could I have left and gone so far away? How could I abandon one daughter for another? What am I doing here?"

I was about to fall deep into a pit of guilt when an answer to those questions rose up from inside me, "Wait a minute. I didn't get here in a vacuum. I didn't call myself to adopt a child and God knows I never planned on going to China. God called me and Rob. Those whom He calls he equips."[ix]

First, I changed my line of thought and began meditating on the whole truth. We had not abandoned Gabrielle but had planned and prepared for our being separated. She was safe with her grandparents and had plenty of support from family, friends and teachers. I had written over 40 letters for Gabrielle to open each morning and night. I'd also bought us a special mother daughter necklace to wear and we were communicating by video twice a day.

Then, I began recounting our adoption process from the start right up until the present moment. Neither Rob nor I thought about adoption prior to God calling us. We did not try to manipulate a desire of our own and label it as a calling from God. My own conscience was clear on this matter and the enemy could not convict me through guilt.

We had a very definite beginning to our journey. It originated one Sunday morning as Rob and I watched a short video about two orphanages in Thailand our church operates through Asia's Hope. Spontaneously we both were given the desire to adopt and thought we were supposed to adopt a child from one of those orphanages. We set up a meeting with one of our Pastors who conveyed these children could not be adopted internationally.

We were deflated by this news wondering if we were meant to proceed. Maybe we had not really heard from God. Keep in mind these types of thoughts are a very subtle form of temptation. Our enemy longs to steal what God has given us to do and comes right away to discourage us before the young seed ever has a chance to mature. I think a sure sign you have truly heard from God regarding your purpose is a quick strike of discouragement designed to make you doubt what you heard.

After the meeting with our Pastor I didn't move very fast which made it seem like I was being slow to act on our calling. Instead I spent a lot of time in prayer asking God to confirm He sent us to adopt. I had no desire to step out and do something of this magnitude if He did not initiate it.

Not everything we do in life requires such confirmation from God. We are called to do many things by the Word which become natural extensions of maturing faith. We can help orphans, widows, and anyone in need God places before us without the need to be "called" to do it. Sometimes we can do this with minimal time and effort. But if God has called you to do something life altering requiring endurance and obedience then I believe there is nothing wrong with seeking His wisdom to help you work through the change about to come <u>as long as you act when it's time.</u>

Jesus spent time preparing His disciples. He told them they would suffer and be persecuted. While blinded God prepared Paul (then Saul) with what he would suffer on account of the name of Jesus. Jesus Himself was prepared from before the foundation of the world for his ministry and was not unaware of the way in which He would lay down His life.

Preparation is necessary for us to follow God properly but it's probably our least favorite thing to do. Preparing for anything takes time but time is what we'd all like God to take out of the equation. We want the glory without the sweat.

But if we would take the time to really inquire of God as to what His plans are for us we would be more at peace and could rest more in our calling instead of being anxious over the details. Knowing you have been called and placed in a position by the Highest Authority gives you much more confidence to do what is before you. Those who call themselves into positions will always be insecure fighting for legitimacy.

If I could describe my prayers after meeting with our Pastor, I'd say I desired more than a calling. I was waiting for the enabling power of God to be revealed to me in my calling. The Gospel is not made up of just words as Paul said but of power. I believed because God called me and Rob then He would also enable us. The enabling power of God is important because with God's power in hand we could not fail! We could count on Him to supply us with everything needed to overcome every obstacle. As our story plays out this was an integral conviction to have and one I could not have defeated my enemy without.

Naturally as I prayed doubts of whether I could love another child as much as Gabrielle came to my mind. I wondered if my heart was big enough to raise a child not my own. It is one thing to be emotional and want to help orphans but quite another to commit to mothering a precious life.

Sometimes we get confused by emotions and step into a calling which is not our own. Since I would be dealing with a child- a human life- I knew the stakes were higher. I could not get into the middle of this and discover I had nothing in me to see it through. I needed to know if I was doing a "good thing" or if it was a "God thing". Believe it or not there is a world of difference between doing something good and something good that originates from God.

Doing good things – especially those things we are emotional about can seem like the right thing to do but they can still turn out wrong. For instance at one point in my life I felt as if God was calling me to start my own business. Every time I acted on this belief nothing ever worked out. Yet time and again this idea kept surfacing. I was a giver of tithes and offerings and thought if I could control my financial destiny a little more, I would be wealthier and have the ability to give even more.

One night when Rob was out of town on business I was praying and became very emotional. I strongly felt these emotions were God's way of giving me the go ahead to buy a machine needed to start a business. I failed in starting a home based business before but I was sure this time it would all work out. I ordered the machine for seventeen hundred dollars. I did my best to make a go of the business but as you can guess the idea didn't take off. I ended up selling the machine on EBay for a fraction of what I paid for it.

There was nothing wrong with my desire to give more financially into God's kingdom. In fact you might think it a noble idea and harbor this belief yourself. But you will eventually come face to face with your true motives and have to decide if you want to do something good or if you want to do the something good which comes from God. Through prayer I came to see my real motive for wanting a business was to become rich having money of my own and being proud I could give more at church. Also I was looking at others. I saw their success in owning a business and thought I could just claim their purpose for myself.

God allowed me to make mistakes knowing in the process I would have to seek Him for my real purpose in Christ. Over the course of time I did and one day wrote a prayer listing all the things I wanted more than money- even a million dollars. At the top of my list was raising a child who loved God.

Writing out this prayer released me to give up on something good my soul deeply desired which was to own a business and be wealthy. It's not that God didn't want wealth for me, He just had another way in mind: "Seek Him first and then all of the things I needed would be given to me." Since then, I haven't had to work myself to the bone nor have I lacked any good thing.

Another example of how emotions can lead us astray and sidetrack our real purpose happened to me at church one Sunday morning. The teen group performed a dramatic skit and I became very emotional while watching. I thought about the deep need in our community to help hurting teens and see them changed by the love of God. There was nothing wrong with this thought but again, I was overcome by my emotions. I almost told the Pastor after service I wanted to become the youth pastor. I had just spent several months working with some of these teens and this request would not have seemed totally out of place.

While being a youth pastor would have been a good -even worthy thing for me to do- it did not originate with God. The thought came from my own prideful, soulish emotions. Prior to this skit I'd spent several months directing a portion of the teen ministry but knew I had a very specific calling and therefore when my portion ended- so did my calling for the teen ministry. So, being used to serving in ministry I felt a little lost. And guilty because I wasn't leading or participating in ministry even though I had a gut feeling this was by design.

It was prideful for me to think I could jump in and run a teen ministry better than it was already being done. Pride has the potential to get us in a lot of trouble by stepping out of our true purpose and the anointed area we have been given. For instance, from the Bible, King Uzziah became prideful after the good things he had done for the Kingdom. Because of pride, he thought he could "do it all" and despite warnings of God sent through others, he did what was the job of the priest (one who held a position of authority given by God to minister in a specific way). Because of his refusal to listen and repent he was struck with leprosy and died.

He crossed a line and could no longer be used by God. It was not his gifting, talent, or desire to accomplish good which was his downfall. It was his own prideful lust to do it all – like the thoughts we have thinking we can do something as well or better than someone else who has authority from God – which got him into trouble. This may be a particular area to watch for if you are administratively gifted. You may see how to do things more efficiently, or see where your gifts could be used to advance a ministry and think it's your job to jump in and take over. If this is you, with your hand involved in way more things than you can possibly juggle in life – please look at what you're doing. If you have not been given the purpose and authority by God its possible Pride has put you in the path of doing what is another's to do. As long as you stand in the way, they may never rise up.

Thankfully, I went home without speaking to my Pastor after service. I took those emotions to God in prayer and worked through an awkward time where I did not serve in ministry. Instead I waited on God to bring forth something for me to do. If I had jumped in head first I would have overstepped the boundaries of who God created me to be and would have had no passion or endurance to lead a teen ministry. The whole thing would have ended miserably for me and others.

I hope you can see by these examples knowing yourself and being able to judge the ideas and emotions coming from within is an important aspect to following Christ. There will always be good things we'd like to do and some things even seem right to do <u>but they are not always what we have been purposed to do</u>. Our good intentions are not always a calling. Wanting to help is not always a reason to do so. At least not if you desire a true calling with authority. True positions of authority are for those who release the pride associated with their own ideas and humble themselves to hear from God and only do what He shows them to do.

Getting back to my adoption story, a couple of months passed while I was praying. One January morning as I was reading a book by Lisa Bevere entitled, "Lioness Arising" my heart was touched by her work to help orphans and rescue women from human trafficking around the world. Interrupting my reading the Lord posed a question to me, "Have you not considered it was Me who sent you the call to adopt?" My answer was simply, "No, Lord". Based on the tone of the question how could my answer have been anything else?

God then revealed to me He placed an open call from the Throne to earth for all who would hear: the time was now to adopt His orphans. Rob and I were one couple of many to hear the call and it was time for me to stop praying and get going. From this encounter and conversation my doubts were totally erased and I knew I had what I was praying for. The call to adopt had not come from me but God and we had the power to accomplish His will. I went straight to my computer and found an adoption agency which had not shown up in my searches before. I gave them a call to begin the process and the rest is history.

If I had not moved instantly and instead continued to labor in prayer over whether God called us or not I may have let God's plan for our lives die prematurely. There comes a point when you must act on what you hear or bear the consequences of an unanswered call.

Now my thoughts turn toward you because you will face a test of your calling. Whatever it is God called you to may require you to give up everything – especially your comfort in order to accomplish His will. It only makes sense to be sure of your calling in this case. Knowing you're called by God for a specific purpose is like laying a strong foundation for a building. It's a basic step not to be ignored if you want to be successful in building something to withstand weight (pressure).

Jesus was attacked many times over his calling to be the Messiah. If He doubted being called of God since before the foundation of the world his whole ministry would have crumbled. His calling was something he had to <u>know</u> and <u>own</u> because it was going to carry him through great spiritual pressure, mental anguish and the physical pain of crucifixion.

While you are on your way to fulfilling God's calling you will have to withstand pressure. <u>Knowing</u> you are specifically called will help you answer your inner doubts. <u>Owning</u> your calling will keep you from giving up too easily and give you a strong weapon to fight spiritual battles.

Spiritual battles are times when you are engaged with a real enemy that is spiritual not physical. You are not warring with low level devils over whether or not you get the closest parking space to the front door of Walmart. You may feel fear as if a physical attacker were present because you are contending and wrestling with systems of power, master spirits who are the world rulers of this present darkness, and spirit forces of wickedness in the spiritual sphere.[x]

Your war is over mind sets, un-holy thoughts and actions striving against a Holy God. It is a real battle with real consequences attached to your victory or loss. Jesus has already won the battle over Satan and his domain but God has chosen you and me - the church, to experience this same victory:

- ❖ "So now through the church the multifaceted wisdom of God [in all its countless aspects] might now be made known [revealing the mystery] to the [angelic] rulers and authorities in the heavenly *places*." [xi]

For this reason you cannot fight with weapons you physically pick up. You need mighty weapons from God to pull down strongholds.[xii]

You can recognize a spiritual attack at the onset if you are feeling discouraged for no reason. Discouragement of this kind may lead to losing hope in God, feeling pressure to give up on something He's told you to do, or make you feel like you can't trust God or His Word.

In my case, I was being questioned about my trust in God and the weapon God gave me to use was Truth.[xiii] The accusation of me "not being a good mother" was a smokescreen to get me to think about an underlying question the enemy poses to all of God's people: "Why are you having so much trouble if you're really called and in the will of God?".

The implication from our spiritual enemy is those who are called by God will never deal with any trouble or face hardships. This is simply not Biblical. If we meditate on our troubles too much though, we can become jealous of others, doubt our calling and begin to undermine our own God given purpose.

Reading the book of Matthew you'll find times when Jesus sent his disciples on missions without him. One time he sent them to preach the Good News and they came back rejoicing, "Even demons are subject to us". Jesus corrected them quickly and told them they should instead rejoice because their names were written in the Book of Life.

Another time Jesus sent them ahead of him to the other side of the sea so he could dismiss a large crowd. The disciples encountered such a fierce storm they thought they would die and were soon terrified seeing Jesus walking on the water towards them. Jesus rebuked the storm and seeing Nature obey His voice they worshipped him.

One experience found them elated on a spiritual high; another time they felt fear with their faith lacking. Both times they were <u>called</u> and <u>sent</u> by Jesus who being God knew what they would encounter. He is the Author and Completer of our faith. He knows how we need to be tested to cause our faith to grow stronger and lead us into a greater dependence upon His Person.

The fact you are going through a trial or test of your calling is not necessarily signaling your faith is weak but perhaps God is perfecting it. If your faith is to be as pure gold what else besides the fire of testing will make it so? It's not so much God needs to know you believe him. It's you who needs to know beyond a shadow of doubt what you are doing did not originate with you.

There is also a matter of glory. Who deserves the glory for your victory? When you are tested regarding your calling you'll walk away with a deep knowing God has and will provide everything you need in your journey out of His great treasury. He has called you and therefore you can be sure it's not up to you to use your own strength to make anything happen.

> ❖ "And we know [with great confidence] that God [who is deeply concerned about us] causes all things to work together [as a plan] for good for those who love God, to those who are called according to His plan *and* purpose."[xiv]

His design and purpose is to have the image of Christ formed within us and in the process lay down our own lives and humbly start walking in the way He leads. You may not be able to understand every part of God's call but while you are praying with expectancy for His direction keep doing what you know to do right now.

May God strengthen and secure you in your calling and may you fulfill His excellent plans and purposes for your life.

LIGHT FROM A DARK NIGHT

6 Battle for Your Dream

Feeling secure in our calling and purpose for being in China I knew Gabrielle would be alright and rolled over in bed to look at Bella. The hotel was out of cribs so we made a little bed between us surrounded by pillows for her. She was sleeping so peacefully. I was amazed she had taken to us so well and didn't seem to be afraid of all the changes taking place in her life.

I thought back to the first time I'd seen a picture of her six months ago. It was a black and white photo when she was five months old. So many wonderful emotions came forward as I looked at her picture the night of her referral. I was incredulous with the feeling our dreams for another child and a sister for Gabrielle were just about ready to come true. Memories of that night continued to float through my mind.

Our consultant said she couldn't believe Bella was even listed as a special needs child. Her medicals were great and all she had was a Mongolian spot on her back and birthmark under her nose. She did have some other darker spots on the back of her thighs and that was it. Our consultant told us to sleep on it before we made a decision but truthfully our minds were already made up. She was going to be our little girl and we accepted her on the spot so the paperwork could get started.

As is customary with foreign adoptions the opinion of an adoption specialist physician is required. They look over all the known medical information and give their best opinion whether the child is healthy enough to adopt. Our physician looking over the medicals saw the black and white picture and thought Bella had a zinc deficiency. She said this was causing the skin discoloration on the back of her thighs. Zinc drops would easily correct it. The orphanage was contacted and said they had the drops and would give them to Bella. We felt really good she had minor issues and were expecting the zinc drops to clear up the darker patches on her skin.

Imagine our surprise when we bathed her and discovered the discolored areas were all over both her legs front and back. We'd seen her legs from the front only once. We forwarded those pictures on to our adoption physician who thought the spots we saw on her legs were healing from something. I started to mentally list all the things we needed medical answers for. She had oozing, crusty sores on the top of her head which bled. She had sores and scabs all over her body. She had whitehead pimply bumps on her hands and deep gauges in the palms of her hands from itching.

We wished we had known more about Bella's medical needs so we'd have been more prepared. We'd done some internet searches while in the hotel room and thought the purple and red patches on her legs were called Port Wine Stains. She definitely did not have a zinc deficiency but with only a black and white photo to go on, I can see why the doctor from the States held this opinion.

I was really hoping to see her doctor at the orphanage. I felt he could give us some answers and fill in the blanks. But more so I just wanted to get her home. As soon as I thought of Bella being home I was hit with another series of yelling from my unseen enemy. "You're never going home with her. Give up the girl. Walk away. (Then you can) go home and don't worry about the lost money. No one would blame you. No one would have to know…."

It was true I felt like I was never going to get home. We had been gone a short time but it seemed like it'd been an eternity. So much happened in a short period of time and my life at home didn't even seem real to me.

What I was being told to do by the screeching demon was to give up the girl- <u>give up Bella</u>. Reject her. Abandon her. Leave her behind and I'd have no trouble getting back home to my life. All hindrances would stop and no one would blame us for not being able to deal with what was happening.

Immediately I responded: "Maybe no one would know but God would". Even if it were possible for no one to know the full story of our experience in China - God would still know. Nothing is ever hidden from God's sight. Not even our hidden thoughts which we might think are secret. God would know if we chose to leave Bella behind and knowing our inner motives – He would know the truth as to why we did it. And on some level we would have to own the defeat associated with coming so close to having our dreams come true only to abort His specific mission for our lives.

With tears streaming down my face I quietly choked out my answer. I was not going to disappoint Jesus Christ, the One I love. Nor was I going to forsake everything He had done to get us this beautiful little girl. I already loved her deeply and was not going to abandon Bella. All the things wrong were superficial and had the potential to be fixed. I was determined to imitate God and bring our little girl out of the lonely darkness she was in into the light where she would step into the love of a family who had been waiting a very long time to bring her home.

We risked everything to follow God and now was not the time to give away our dream and quit. How about you? Have you been praying and believing for a God given dream to come to pass and just as it's about to happen you encounter a circumstance requiring you to make a decision to either step backward or risk everything to go forward? Do you wonder if God really meant to bless you anyway?

I have much to say to you about risking everything to stay with what God has told you to do. I know so much is riding on your decision and I want to say: <u>don't give away God's dream for your life- especially not to your enemy!</u>

Every one of us will be tested regarding the dreams that originate *in Christ* because it's those dreams in particular that are born of faith and can make the most impact in the world. The mission God has given you is the very thing you <u>must do</u>. The enemy seeks to do more than destroy your person; he wants to stamp out the development needed not just to begin a thing but to finish it. Whatever the consequence you must not give away your right to complete the dream God gave to you.

What the enemy wanted me to do was give up on God's desire to expand our family. He wanted me to believe a lie, "no one would know if we rejected Bella" and choose to sin based on a false statement. I will call it sin because all sin is voluntary disobedience. Satan can tempt us and along with temptation bring great pressure to follow his lead but he cannot force us to do anything.

Satan tempted Eve with "Hath God said…" This was a spiritual battle designed to get Eve thinking more about the goodness of the apple rather than the goodness of God. The apple looked good to eat and the command not to eat it didn't seem right or fair. Why would God place something so beautifully tempting in their midst anyway?

In their story I can hear my own questioning thoughts. At times God's words are so contrary to my own and I pause to question whether I've heard Him correctly. It's in these moments I absolutely must take my stand on what God said and turn from looking at the circumstance causing me to doubt. We must win the spiritual side of things first then we can win with faith filled actions.

Eve lost the spiritual battle first then committed an act of sin which altered the destiny of all creation. She did not stand on the command given to Adam "they should not eat the fruit from the tree of the knowledge of good and evil" and therefore could not resist the temptation of Satan.

Because they were united as husband and wife they had a joint calling and were enabled by God to resist the devil. This calling and enablement would have been passed down to their children and to every generation afterwards including us. So when it comes to spiritual battles we cannot think their outcome is unimportant but must keep in mind when we win in God's name then so do our descendants in some way.

Last chapter I shared with you how I overcame the battle of my calling by knowing it was God who called us to adopt and thus being sure everything would work out according to His plan and not mine. Therefore, with my calling settled I could stand on a strong foundation and choose to follow my dream when presented with an opportunity to sin (voluntarily disobey God based on circumstances).

Not all sin has an evil appearance. Many times as Eve discovered sin can look good. We can do all the reasoning we want and attach all the right spiritual approvals onto our desiring something wrong which appears good. We've even been taught to go to the Word and find a Scripture to "cover us" not because we love God or desire sanctification but because we want something and feel if we have a Scripture verse to back it up then God is obligated to comply. In this case we are in serious error and are being defeated without even knowing it.

The tree Eve ate from was the Tree of the knowledge of <u>good and evil</u>. The good from this tree was just as bad as the evil and was and still is not like the good we can have from partaking of Christ who is The Tree of Life. It's important to learn to distinguish if the good thing that's got our attention is really from God or not. If it is not then Satan has tempted you to stray from your God given path. And while you may be blessed on a parallel path in some way because God loves you, your inner man will nag you with the feeling there is something different you should be doing. And there is, but you will have to go back to the fork in the road where you voluntarily chose another path.

My point in looking into this is two-fold. For one, being in the heat of the moment you could make hasty decisions so the pain and aggravation of your trial will stop. But enduring the pain of your trial by faith is what God uses to develop your character so you can complete the goal of your faith.[xv]

Secondly, you'll have to discern what type of good you are being presented with because you have enough time in life to fulfill God's good plan not your own. You simply don't have the time to spend doing "it all" just because you can. It's true there are many good things you could devote your time to and they are not bad or sinful in and of themselves. But if you follow too many of these little tributaries because they look good and might be fun to do you'll lose sight of what should be the main stream of your life and wind up confused.

Satan and his crew have been busy and Christians are rightly exasperated with all the bad in the world but we cannot join every cause and focus on all of it. It is not our job to save the world; Jesus Christ has already done this. Our job is to abide *in* Him and let His life flow through us with power at the proper time and place. He is the one who gives us life and power to do those things prepared in advance for us to do.

Maybe you are living abiding in the Vine. If so, life is becoming clearer and more light is being shed into your heart and onto your path. You probably feel more confident in what you're doing because you can "see" more spiritually and don't have to exert so much energy of your own. God's life is flowing through you and the stream you are in is getting wider. This stream is your life in Christ. As it expands so does your ability to reach and restore others. You've laid down your life and expectations and now you can say God's desires and dreams are yours. It's not so much you won't ever encounter tests or trials abiding in Christ but your reactions and outcomes will be different.

If you are not abiding in Christ, you'll feel uneasy, in the dark a lot and be confused over what you should be doing. Chances are you are doing more things with the hopes some of it is right and pleasing to God. Doing things which seem right and even good are not really godly good if your spiritual and family life are in disarray. Doing good you are not specifically called or equipped to do doesn't cover you for lack of relationship with God and family. No ministry, no matter how good you think it is – is worth losing your prayer time, spouse or children for.

Christian service is not a replacement for relationship with God. You aren't close to God because you are serving in ministry at church or giving to a ministry doing what it was called to do. You are close to God through communion with His Son. You become closer as you talk with Him and hear His voice. To pursue intimacy you might have to drop some of the balls you are bouncing. You can't be God effectively but you can effectively be you. This you, the real you, is the one who bears the dreams of God and by faith brings them into being. Those are the dreams flowing in your main stream which you have exactly the right amount of time and energy to see through.

So, use caution when presented with doing something good especially if it requires a great deal of time and takes you off of a path you know God placed you on. Make no mistake, the enemy of your soul wants you to fear him and human rejection more than you reverence God and his plans for your life. The satanic spirit wants you to make quick emotional decisions you think are right and will please others. Evil forces create intense emotional pressure around you to crowd out peaceful conversation with God and will demand you make a decision immediately without inquiring of the Holy Spirit. This is one way the pride of life and all that is evil in the heart of man come forth with wrong motives to do what is seen as good in the world. But what is seen as good in the world will pass away and come to nothing.

I can almost hear you wondering what all this has to do with battling for your dream. I feel like I have to answer a couple questions and take some things off your plate before you can move forward. The first question is: "Can I do good things for others without being called?" The second is: "I am doing a good work- people are being helped. Who will do all the ministry work if I don't?"

Of course you can do kind things for others without a calling. But even an unsaved person knows how to be kind and help others. God gave all humanity a spirit of love so loving others whether we know Christ as savior or not is truly wired into the fiber of our being.

I'm talking about those things you get yourself tangled up in which steal your time away from being the woman you were created to be.

You'll never know <u>her</u> – the inner woman you long to be - unless you lay down everything of your own doing and follow Christ. How many of us feel like we couldn't do one more thing or our life would just break apart. We are women with big hearts and don't like to see needs go unfilled if we think we have what it takes to step in. Here is a revelation though. God is not an evil task master who demands you give your life to the point of loss and exhaustion. He is kind, gentle and deeply loves you. His yoke is easy. He holds the dream life you must intensely fight for and once found you must use the same intensity to protect it.

This fight is never over "stuff". Ultimately it's not things we're after like a car or new home. Rather it's your spiritual life which is being blocked by Satan. It's the life of power he wants you to be too busy to live in.

If you remain disconnected from the Vine, a stubborn branch who goes its own way, you may be cut off. Being cut off as a life not connected to the Vine will be tough. You may have received a call from God which stands and will never be taken away. But it's the <u>commissioning</u> of this call you won't ever receive and may find somewhere, someone in the body of Christ is or will be doing what you felt was yours to do.

If you feel that this woman is you, if God is touching your heart right now then I implore you to take action right away. It is not too late for you to stop the runaway train which seems to be your life and begin ordering your steps towards the path God would have you to be on in this season. On the other side of the mountain is something to fulfill you in a way like nothing has ever been able to do. It will be given to you by God, you can't earn it and won't feel like you deserve it. It's going to cost you your self-led life but to gain your life in Christ is a treasure worth fighting for.

As far as all the work needing done in ministry and so forth I think the best answer is to let it be done by those who are abiding in the Vine and have been given life and power to do it. If there is no one given the ability by God to do a particular task then maybe it's not something which should be done at this time. It may be a good work but if you are doing it without any commission from God it is a dead, religious work for you.

Recognizing emotions, distractions, and unusual circumstances leading you toward voluntarily giving up on the dream and plan of God for you as a spiritual battle, is a step in the right direction. First win in the area of your calling. It's your foundation and if strong you'll be able to rest the weight of pressure on it and your dream won't crumble from testing and temptations. Then choose to turn away from all occasions to sin and continue doing what God called you to do.

Now, I'd like to say something about hindrance. The enemy raging against me implicated he was controlling our situation and had the power to stop all hindrances if I would give Bella back to the orphanage. However, I believe every hindrance was placed strategically in my path just so we'd arrive to pick up the perfect child for us <u>at the appointed time</u>. I'm of the opinion God is in charge of my life and yours and He can use hindrance no matter where it is coming from for His good purposes.

Satan and his evil horde are sneaky and will not play fair. According to Jesus, Satan is the father of <u>all</u> lies. How sinister was his plan and purpose regarding an orphaned baby; an innocent life who could not fend for herself? Can you see how evil his schemes are even for babies? He wanted us to reject and abandon Bella thereby setting abandonment as a theme for her life. By rejecting his lies I believe a curse was reversed and instead she is holy; sanctified (by having believing parents)[xvi] and set apart to serve God. What the enemy meant for evil in her life- God will use and make good.

And what would have happened to me if I'd said we would send her back to the orphanage? The inference from the enemy was I could go home with no worries not even about lost money. Surely you don't think this is true- do you? Satan knows more about sin than we do. He doesn't leave us alone or stop the pain when we agree to sin. Those are just enticing words to push us over the edge. Consequences just continue on in other forms. I would have been relieved of momentary difficulty but I would not be able to escape grief, loss and regret. And my original desire for another child would still remain but who knows if the opportunity to adopt a child would come again.

Years ago I found myself in a similar battle when I was going through a difficult pregnancy with our daughter Gabrielle. The Holy Spirit clearly showed me if I didn't fight the (spiritual) battle which was the fear of miscarriage and win; I would certainly miscarry and continue to be on the outside of my desire looking in. If I lost this child I would find myself still praying for a miracle child I could have had now. You see it was my Now time, my appointed time to be pregnant even though it was difficult. If I didn't recognize God's plan for me and fight for it, there was no guarantee I would become pregnant again.

All of us should be on the lookout for snares of the enemy designed to steal the answer to prayer by having us focus on an unfavorable circumstance. But please, if you have lost a child do not feel this is a word of condemnation saying you didn't have enough faith. This was a very specific word from the Lord <u>for me</u>. I needed to be rattled because I wasn't taking ownership of the fight in prayer. I wanted to give up yet I wanted my unborn child to fight for her life from the womb.

So if you are in the fight of your life right now in any battleground use this word and fight for your miracle. If you don't it may be a while before an opportunity comes your way again. Or it may be this is it. Don't let your dream pass by. You take ownership of the battle.

Lastly, I would like you to see one more scheme Satan might try to use against you. An answered prayer. Again, I'll go back to my pregnancy with Gabrielle. When I first found out I was pregnant (after fifteen years of marriage and six years of intense prayer for a child), you'd think I would have been ecstatic. But I wasn't. I was strangely quiet, somber and felt a heaviness around me. I was afraid of getting too excited because I didn't feel quite right. What if I were to tell everyone I was pregnant and lose the baby? I'd feel like a fool for saying God had given me a miracle.

There will always be an element of risk present with every fight. Do we believe God or not? Should we believe God even if it doesn't turn out the way we want it to? Those are questions we must answer which will wind up increasing our faith.

Thankfully I happened to have a dear mentor to rely on during this time. One night after a mid-week church service I told her I was tired of praying and didn't have any strength left. I wanted her to pray for me – to take the burden off me.

But as was her custom all she had to say was, "Mmmm…" and I knew I'd better rethink what I'd just said. She told me to look up Isaiah 66:9 and see what God had to say. Please read it carefully and see what God would say to you in regard to trusting Him with your dream.

- ❖ "Shall I bring to the moment of birth and not give delivery?" says the LORD.
  "Or shall I who gives delivery shut *the womb*?" says your God.[xvii]

This is not just a word for women about to give birth to a physical child. It is for everyone who will allow God to place life inside knowing you will birth something of purpose greater than yourself. It will not always be easy – even when it's God who ignites the process. It's still you who has to endure and use your will to determine crossing the finish line is worth it.

You cannot always count on others to pray for you. It's not whether they want to or have an anointing to pray but it's more about you drawing nearer to God. Even if it seems like you've lost by the standards of this world – whether a life or a dream – just stay focused on drawing closer to Christ. He will show you the Heavenly side of things and you may be surprised to discover what is loss on earth may be gain in eternity.

Keep your mind on His timing and pathway and know he will not birth a dream in you and then shut every door before you without opening a new one. Be ready to jump on a different path or a newly opened door like we did when switching our adoption country from Bulgaria to China. What looked like the disappointing end of our journey was really the beginning.

If you've failed in the past and given the enemy more ground than you'd like by all means grieve over any lost opportunity. There is a type of Godly grief that will lead you into a much better place spiritually than carrying around guilt for any length of time.

I doubt you've found this book on a whim. Instead, I believe God sent you to read about my experiences in order to see your own in a clearer light. Find a way to set your mind on course to become closer to Christ than ever before. He is more important to know and will fill your soul deeper than the accomplishment of any dream can. He's the Author (the beginning) and the finisher (the accomplisher) of your faith.[xviii] Your purpose is found in Him and you can be sure it is just what your soul has been longing for.

I'm praying for you to succeed in your spiritual battles. I hope you too will carry your dream born of faith over the threshold into a place of fulfillment. Only you and God know the path you've taken to get to where you are. Be steadfast; He has a beautiful ending to your long journey.

LIGHT FROM A DARK NIGHT

7 Battle for Your Strength in Christ

By now it was the middle of the night and I had fought two spiritual battles. I wanted to get some sleep knowing I'd have a long day ahead of me taking care of Rob and Bella. I wasn't interested in fighting anymore and thought if I ignored the evil presence he would sense my disinterest and leave me alone.

I picked up my IPad and saw some new email messages. One of my closest friends sent a note she was praying for me. She said I was, "a strong woman of God and would get through this time". My immediate thought was, "If I'm so strong how come I don't feel like it?" I felt needy. I rarely asked for prayer from my friends but knew I could not face what was coming against me alone. I was praying but surviving also which was taking an enormous amount of my energy.

As I was thinking about my friends a new torrent of screams from my unseen enemy yelled, "You aren't strong because your faith is only good where you're comfortable", and "Your faith isn't real".

I began to ask myself a very tough series of questions. Was my faith real? Did I only do things I felt comfortable doing? Was I really living my life by faith? Had I been leading others out of my strength and not God's? I was nagged by the fact I'd felt like a strong woman of faith before we'd left for China but now I felt weak. Was there truth to what my enemy said?

Suddenly from within my heart I heard, "Let the weak say I am strong". I recognized those words as a verse from a song I'd sung many times as a child in church. I got up and walked to the bathroom so I could close the door and have some privacy to pray aloud. I was bothered because I didn't know if this song verse was in the Bible. I asked God if this was the answer to my enemy's accusations then I needed Him to confirm it with a scripture I did know. Right away these words from the Apostle Paul came to mind:

❖   "If I must boast, I will boast of the things that reveal my weakness [the things by which I am made weak in the eyes of my opponents]."[xix]

❖   "So I am well pleased with weaknesses, with insults, with distresses, with persecutions, and with difficulties, for the sake of Christ; for when I am weak [in human strength], then I am strong [truly able, truly powerful, truly drawing from God's strength]."[xx]

Those words penetrated my soul and a wave of God's love washed over me. I found myself crying as my life was laid bare before God and I could see the worthlessness of doing anything out of my own strength ever again. I wasn't sure why God brought this to my attention on this night but right then and there I decided I'd rather be a weak woman, one who is humble before God instead of being proud of my own self, so His strength would reign in and over my life.

I began repenting of <u>the need to be strong in life </u>(living out of my own abilities and strength) and many of my life experiences came to mind. As each one surfaced I asked God to forgive me for counting on myself and my own abilities instead of His. While I was at it I poured out my Self, asking for forgiveness of anything standing in the way of being close to Him. I didn't quit until the images from my life stopped and I sensed the Holy Spirit had accomplished all he desired in my soul.

I stood up and looked at myself in the mirror and could tell the night had taken its toll on me. It was time to get my day started so I could do a video chat with Gabrielle and the family before Bella woke up. Somehow through this night I became sure I needed to stay in Nanjing with Rob while he was sick. I would not travel to Bella's orphanage and would rest my hope in God to help us.

I continued mulling over in prayer what the Lord revealed to me during the night. Absolutely nothing changed in my outward circumstances. Everything looked the same as before only I was a totally different woman inside. I felt clean - completely empty of my Self. And pure - at perfect peace with my inner being.

I had no idea why the revelation of being empty of Self and needy before God was so important or why it was necessary for me to see my own weakness. Looking back on my experience I have evidence of this verse, "…the Lord knows how to rescue the godly out of temptations and trials…"[xxi] God, knowing my future prepared me in advance. For in one week the ultimate test of my faith would come and I would need the victories of this night to stand firm.

We have so much of Christ to apprehend and appropriate in our lives and this is the greatest work we can be involved with. We're living in perilous even evil times when human life is being snuffed out by those who live in and get their direction from deep darkness. There is much to be seen yet we don't see or cannot see because it is out of the realm of our natural and/or spiritual sight. This is not the time to casually glance at God keeping him an arms distance away. Now is a time we should be pressing in to the Light and requiring Him as much as the air we breathe.

For years my inner prayer life had been leading me to see and know the emptiness and vanity of Self so the Holy Spirit could reveal Christ to me in this area. This is what true sanctification is: an inner, personal work accomplished between you and the Holy Spirit. Only He knows when your soul is ready to be emptied out and Christ poured in.

The fullness of Christ cannot dwell in a soul who is full of itself. After the enemy made accusations against me my own soul began asking itself the question, "Why do I feel so needy?" If I had not allowed myself to search out the emptiness of my own self and instead ignored the question, I would not have been given the opportunity by the Holy Spirit to know Christ as my sufficiency and complete strength.

As I wrote you in the beginning my writing isn't meant to keep you from your own dark night of the soul. I'm writing so you may recognize your inner work as being important and necessary for the increasing of your faith. The internal pressure you feel now will lead you to increased knowledge of God and yourself and will give you the resolve to keep on following Him no matter the cost.

Each of us needs to work out our own salvation. Salvation in this sense is not where you'll spend eternity so much as the work of salvation leading you to be transformed into the image of Christ. We do not own this work by reading about it or listening to a pastoral message on sanctification. We own it by submitting ourselves to the Holy Spirit and allowing the process no matter the internal pain. The desire of our hearts is for a manifestation of Christ. We want the experience of His saving grace for ourselves in every area of life and many times this comes through trials of various kinds.

I was about to write the Holy Spirit is gentle in leading you to discover yourself and He is but it won't feel gentle all the time. Sometimes you'll feel like God is trying to kill you. Of course He's not really killing you just your inner Self who is trying to keep you from deferring to God's will at all times. If you identify with this then you need to know there is something beautiful on the other side of what you're going through. You are about to know Christ in a new way and produce something eternal - the fruit of holiness.

The first step toward apprehending Christ is to see ourselves living out of our own strength as being flawed. We have to <u>feel</u> and <u>see the need</u> for Christ to save us from living life out of our own strength before we can ever know His saving touch of strength. Feeling secure in our own abilities or strength is serious error for the Christian because we are to depend on Christ alone and see his strength as sufficient for our lives. If not, we are looking at committing a sin of pride.

- ❖ "For all that is in the world—the lust *and* sensual craving of the flesh and the lust *and* longing of the eyes and <u>the boastful pride of life [pretentious confidence in one's resources or in the stability of earthly things]</u>—these do not come from the Father, but are from the world."[xxii]

To live a life of faith we should be on guard against the pride of life. Being secure in our ability or the ability of others to provide the necessary resources needed to fulfill the will of God is a worldly idea. It is easy in the U.S.A. to rely on our own resources and our own abilities. We have so much at our disposal: internet, medicine, books - you name it. If I had never gone to a country where I felt like I had nothing, I wouldn't have known how much I'd come to rely on myself and the things of the world.

God's ways are so different from ours. For the growing of our faith He might tell us to do things which go against the grain of our human nature. He might tell us to love when we want to hate. He might tell us to endure when we want to give up. He might say stand still when we want to move.

It's totally against my nature to write about my weaknesses and failings because I want you to know I'm strong. But just who is my strength in? Anyone can be confident in their own self or be strong inside. But not everyone can be weak completely relying on another for their strength. Sounds an awful lot like being a baby who cannot do anything for their own self until they grow up a bit. If we have felt like we had to be strong, in our own strength, it's time to go back to being a baby before God and learn how to rely on him again. In hearing about my weakness and seeing how my life has worked out then you can be amazed at God's goodness instead of thinking I just have it all together.

Does being weak mean we have to accept everything life throws at us? Of course not. It's okay to pray asking God to remove obstacles and our prayers are powerful to affect things. But if He allows something to remain you may need to be open to the idea of a greater work being done in you than you can understand right now.

Look at this powerful promise to those who decide to be weak to the flesh, the world and to Satan:

> ❖ But He said to me, My grace (My favor and loving-kindness and mercy) is enough for you [sufficient against any danger and enables you to bear the trouble manfully]; for *My* strength *and* power are made perfect (fulfilled and completed) *and* [a]*show themselves most effective* in [your] weakness. Therefore, I will all the more gladly glory in my weaknesses *and* infirmities, that the strength *and* power of Christ (the Messiah) may rest (yes, may [b]pitch a tent over and dwell) upon me![xxiii]

Christ's strength and power are made perfect in our weakness. I have been turning this phrase over and over inside myself. What would change in our lives if we saw our weaknesses as areas potentially made perfect by Christ's strength and power?

I can't tell you how many times I cried out when we first got back from China -"God help me!" We had an unexpected hard transition with Gabrielle who was deeply hurt by us leaving her at home. She expressed her anger more with me than Rob. After putting the girls to bed I stayed in their room to pray. I silently yelled out to God in the darkness, "Make it better or make it go away". But He allowed the situation to remain. And so, the future of our family is a matter of my faith to rely on His strength and not my own.

I've been honest writing you how hard it's been and have let you in on my inner struggles so you will be able to give God glory when you see how his strength has made everything perfect. If all you really see is a perfect me how could you be encouraged by my faith? What faith would you see if you didn't know any of my struggles?

Isn't this how we relate to men and women of the Bible? Initially we identify with them through their flaws and pain. But then we want to know and connect with the God who sees beyond human imperfections for ourselves. Through His faithfulness they were brought to a place of comfort. God will comfort and faithfully carry you beyond your human failings and limitations too. Be encouraged to keep pressing forward in Christ.

I think we have become good at hiding things from our Christian friends. We hide because we're afraid to appear weak in our faith. And there is not a lot of understanding about the nature of trials and the importance of them for the health of our souls. The Apostle Paul has an entire discourse on being weak and strong and as Christian brothers how we are to relate to one another.

In strength we are not to hurt weaker brothers through our actions. In weakness we are not to think strong brothers are not following Christ because we don't understand their growth. In all things we should be careful not to allow secrecy or darkness to be a cover for anything in our lives. I think we could try to look deeper at the trials of our sisters in Christ and recognize God may be at work on a deeper level than can be seen or known by us. Real faith can be messy and some who are suffering are doing so not because of sin but because of the goodness and purity of their lives. Let's be the kind of women who know how to discern the difference.

As I continue my story you will see how important being empty of my self and full of Christ's strength will become in the ultimate testing of my faith. Just so you know, when I speak of being "empty of self" I am not saying we should be empty for the sake of being empty or void of everything which makes us unique. The Holy Spirit is our guide and again, all emptiness of Self including our self-will <u>must not remain empty but must be filled with Christ</u>. We should have the expectancy of being filled with Christ or we may be deceived to receive something from Satan.

We cannot orchestrate the healing of our own soul any more than we can save ourselves apart from Jesus Christ. Sometimes it's just hard to see the sin in our own lives and we cry out for God to take all of "us" away so others only see Him. You will have to trust God in this matter. As I've written it may be profitable for others to see the frail part of your faith so they will be encouraged to keep going not striving for perfection sake but for holiness.

It's okay to ask God to <u>take your life and use it</u> for His glory. I've heard Gloria Copeland say this is what she prayed at the beginning of her conversion. From a pure heart she intended to lay down her own life – her own ideas of what life should be like – and asked God to do something with her life instead. She did this from a perspective of humility and was probably led into a time of learning obedience to the Word.

False humility would have had her plunge into utter worthlessness and self-loathing eventually crowding out God's kindness and good plan for her life. God has taken the offering of one's life in the past and done great things with those who from a pure heart have desired His plan over their own. He is the same yesterday, today and forever and can do the same for you no matter where you are in your faith walk.

What's not okay is asking God to <u>take away all of you</u>. If He did this you would cease to exist. God created you and sent you to earth for a purpose. He has no intention of eliminating "all of you" or there would be no purpose to you being alive at all. It's really "all of <u>you</u> -in Christ" He desires.

Once I heard a woman say, "Lord, take my will". She was having a hard time overcoming something and was at the point of exasperation. She just could not give up what she knew she should. She thought if God took over her will she would be free. She didn't want the responsibility anymore. If God took her will surely she could give up something she deeply desired. And if God failed with control of her will then she would be free of blame and guilt. Everything would be God's fault. But, God is not in the business of "taking" the will of human beings. Our will is our own to choose good or evil; life or death. Even the ultimate choice of God or Satan; heaven or hell.

Saying you want God to take your will is really like saying you want God to do the work for you. I know from personal experience how hard it is to overcome things which are deeply rooted in the soul. But, by not going for change when God has given everything needed to overcome is to deny the power of Christ and the Cross to transform you.

From the beginning, God gave man the power to overcome evil desires. Desires that demand mastery over your soul and kill the Spirit of God dwelling in you – which is love. Temptation is hard to deal with. It pulls strongly and comes against you with everything it's got from every angle possible. It flips good and evil so what is wrong looks good and seems right.

If you say you cannot change and are not willing to truly discipline your own mind and flesh – doing whatever it takes – then you will remain powerless. I don't believe being a powerless woman is who you want to be. You'd never read a book like this if it was. Instead, I believe you need encouraged. You need to know: You have not gone too far to change course and live out God's plan for your life.

If you've failed before, repent and come back to God again. Every day if you need to. Be thankful you are alive and try taking it one step at a time. It's just like breathing. We breathe one breath at a time and continue to live. We don't take ten breaths at a time to get us ahead faster.

As I wrote in the beginning, God expects us to win. He knows the power he's placed in us is greater than any other created thing. You give God a very great glory by allowing yourself to bend and defer to His Spirit.

Never give up.

Rise up.

Stand and take your place.

And while this change is making a home within - you will show the goodness of God to all who have ears to hear and eyes to see.

LIGHT FROM A DARK NIGHT

8 Alone in China

I survived my dark night of the soul and was tired from lack of sleep but thankful to see a new day. Rob was not feeling any better and had a temperature of 100.3. With our decision made to stay in Nanjing and separate from the group for a couple days I called our guide with the news. He was disappointed and stopped by the room before leaving to make sure we knew we'd be alone. I knew it all too well as I had been thinking about getting food and water without Rob's help.

The next couple days I kept the room as dark as I could so Rob could sleep. He was feeling so bad and got up a few times but could only sit with his hands over his face. I made good use of my time bonding with Bella during those two days. We had nothing to do but play with a few toys. She was fascinated by a photo book which had pictures of her new home and family members. I held and kissed her showing my deep love. I was meeting her needs quickly to form the best bond possible.

At times I carried her out into the hallway for a change of scenery and ventured downstairs to the lobby once. I was not going out into the mall area by myself. So I made our water last and ordered room service for every meal. I know you might be thinking this sounds ridiculous and from the comfort of my own home it does to me too.

I'm not a person prone to fear but we were in a foreign country – a communist foreign country. I knew none of the language. I did not even have papers showing Bella to be ours. We were all very aware of being guests in China and wanted to display America in the best light possible without any occurrence of something which might hinder our adoptions.

The Chinese people we did interface with were very kind. Like the cleaning ladies who got to know us quite well. Bella wet the bed twice and they came in to change the bedding.

They were so sweet to us and made Bella laugh. Sometime during the day the front desk called to say they'd ordered a crib from another hotel and would bring it right up. I was relieved as I'd now have a safe place to put Bella down for a few minutes.

Rob slept all of Wednesday and on Thursday his fever was gone. He was weak but starting to come out of it. Bella began answering to her new name and some of the sores on her hands were starting to heal. I was using the hydrocortisone cream on her other rash and sores but didn't think it was helping much because she was still scratching like crazy. While the rash was not making any progress Bella's other skills were improving quickly. She could sit and hold her head up without falling forward.

Rob felt well enough to venture out of the room at supper time. We went to the hotel buffet and were the only customers for a while. Rob didn't want to eat anything yet so I walked around looking at the food. I circled the buffet several times as usual not able to find anything for myself to eat. In hindsight I should have asked to eat directly off the room service menu.

That night we had a fun time watching Bella eat. She hyperventilated in between mouthfuls of food. It was her way of saying, "more, more don't stop the food". We spent the rest of the night in our room and squeaked out another day. They were long days for sure but satisfying as we knew Bella was blossoming and adjusting to us well.

9 Moving Forward

It was Friday morning and I met up with the rest of the group for breakfast. They were exhausted mentally and physically from the trip to the girls' orphanage. Some were not feeling well and thought we were the lucky ones to have stayed behind. They said the orphanage was nice and were served a wonderful meal by the staff. The orphanage gave the girls special gifts. One of the gifts was a scrap book with pictures of the orphanage and surrounding area.

It was an emotional trip as they visited the place where their child was abandoned. I had a pang of regret in my stomach at not being able to see this for Bella but when I reflected on how well she was doing with us I had to let it go.

Bella was smiling while eating and one mom was surprised she was answering to her new name already. We hurried through breakfast because we were leaving Nanjing at 1 pm. We had a lot of packing to do. I was glad to be moving forward into the last leg of our trip. Everyone said we'd like Guangzhou because it was warm and more relaxed like Southern Florida. Because of this it was an international tourist destination and catered to Americans.

After a long day of travel we arrived at The Victory Hotel in Guangzhou, China. I liked the name of the hotel because I felt victory was now in sight. We were so close to going home! The air was fresh, warm and balmy just like Miami, Florida. Our room was a small suite with a sitting room and a TV. Our bedroom could be closed off with pocket doors. It was comfortable and felt more like home. A stroller was waiting for us and it would double as a high chair to feed Bella.

Saturday morning arrived with much anticipation as we all had medical appointments for our children. The medicals were very important. The children had to pass them in order to get Visas to exit China and enter the United States. Our Visa appointments were made in advance and our entire trip to China was based around this one appointment. Our Visa appointments were at the U.S. Embassy on Monday so nothing could go wrong today.

We arrived at the medical facility and were taken to a special area for adoptive families. We waited a while and then all of a sudden were called in for our exams and everything became a rush. We had four stations for Bella to go through and hurried through the first three. These stations were nothing more than taking temperature and getting weight and so forth. We had no reason to think Bella wouldn't pass these medicals but the last station proved to be the most difficult for us.

The fourth room had an exam table and a doctor was waiting for us. We had to take Bella's clothes off and to my dismay her skin looked really bad. I could tell the doctor thought so too. I started to sweat and Bella started to cry. The doctor began asking me questions about the bumps on her chest.

Our guide interpreted back and forth. He instructed us in advance to be honest when answering questions but not volunteer too much information

I wanted the doctor to know she came to us with the bumps. They were not any better but they were not worse either. I actually hoped he might be able to help us. He continued to look at Bella and speak in Chinese to our guide. Another doctor was called in to look at Bella and the doctors talked back and forth. I could tell by their body language something was not going well.

The first doctor said he thought Bella had scabies. I asked him what this meant for Rob and me. Through his mask he said adults had nothing to worry about. He prescribed a cream stating we should put it on her skin twice a day for a week. The second doctor thought she had chicken pox. The doctors continued to talk to our guide who suddenly became very animated and told us to wait outside the room. He motioned for us to go way down to the end of the hallway away from everyone else. We became very tense not knowing what was happening.

Our guide came out of the room to talk to the group. He explained because there was a threat of chicken pox from Bella we had to be quarantined immediately. If Bella had chicken pox no one in our group could go home until she was cleared because we'd all been exposed to her. My mind started clicking off the hotel and airfare changes this would cause us all to make. Not to mention everyone had children and jobs waiting on us back home.

The rest of the group took this news well. No one seemed upset but inside I was. I could not bear the thought of being in China longer than what was already planned. I could not be away from Gabrielle any longer. After the bombshell of being quarantined it was time for us to leave the medical building. We could not ride in the same elevator or bus with the rest of the group and took a taxi back to the hotel. We rode in silence. Both of us knew Bella did not have chicken pox but had no way to prove it. We were helpless and wondered how we were going to get out of this one.

Our guide left us at the hotel and went to get the prescription for Bella. He brought it to us but I had an inner feeling we should not use it. I wrote an email to my sister in law and asked her to contact our doctor. Because of the time difference I would have to wait until the following morning for an answer.

Being quarantined meant we could not be seen eating or socializing with anyone from the group if Bella was present. It left us feeling alone and was hard for the group to keep away from us. But it could have been worse. I think our guide knew the doctors and gave them his word we would stay separated. Otherwise they could have quarantined us to a hospital room. Thankfully we were released and allowed to be in our hotel room.

The next day seemed to last forever. Rob went out to get food and water while I stayed in the room with Bella. Being alone in the room again turned out to be in our favor. There was nothing to do but bond. We spread a sheet on the floor and let Bella roll around and explore. She learned to crawl on this sheet which was quite an accomplishment since the week before she couldn't even sit up on her own.

During our quarantine I would become hungrier than ever before. Rob was allowed to go on sightseeing adventures with the group but he had no control of when they would return. I waited for him to bring me food and was treated late one night with a Pizza Hut pizza. Thank God for the American pizza makers being in China! Another time he brought me the best grilled cheese and fries on the planet from Lucy's restaurant.

I lived for the times I could talk to family through Skype. The Wi-Fi in our room didn't work so I talked in the lobby or in front of the elevators. The elevator area was dimly lit with cameras posted in the hallways. It felt like I was in a spy movie.

We waited for word from the States about the scabies cream. The advice from two doctors was "do not use it"! It was double the strength of the same medicine in the U.S. and should only be used one time not twice a day for a week. The medicine was a pesticide and could be dangerous to a baby with any open sores. I thought about the oozing, bleeding sores on Bella's head and could not give her something harmful. Another family in our group lent us their prescription which had the proper U.S. dosage. We gave Bella one application of the cream.

On Sunday amidst all the worry over Bella we needed some fresh air and decided to walk to Starbucks. On our way down to the lobby a young man got on the elevator with us. As we were walking out he gave us the best gift ever. With his hand he motioned to his heart and with broken English said, "What you're doing - wonderful". My eyes filled with tears and I'm so glad God put this young man onto our path. It was just the right moment to be reminded while things were hard - they were not over. This young man quickly helped us connect to our God given purpose to bring Bella home.

Amidst all of your struggles in life, I pray God will put someone on your path to encourage you at just the right moment too.

10 Helpless Not Hopeless

After two days of quarantine Monday morning finally arrived. Our group had 10:30 a.m. Visa reservations at the American Embassy for our children. They did not accept walk ins at the Embassy to adopt a child so this appointment was very important. We were told there was a swearing in ceremony for adoptive families and I bought Bella a special dress for this occasion. However, I opted not to dress her in it because the fabric seemed like it would make her itchy and hot. When Bella was hot the bumps on her skin looked worse and this wouldn't be good today.

Technically we were still under quarantine but were allowed to travel downtown with the group by bus. Everyone headed to the U.S. Embassy while Rob, Bella, our guide and I walked across the street to the medical center. We were going back for Bella to be rechecked and receive medical clearance papers for her visa.

Our guide said this would take about ten minutes and we'd go to the Embassy afterwards. We were nervous heading into the medical building but our guide was confident we'd get our clearance quickly and be able to stay on schedule. Thinking this would be a quick in and out I only took in a couple diapers and wipes leaving everything else on the bus. The U.S. Embassy had strict rules of what could be taken inside and there would be no time to go back to the bus and drop a diaper bag off.

As we neared the top of the steps into the building our guide greeted and began speaking in Chinese to a man he knew. On the elevator our guide introduced him to us as one of the doctors on staff. The doctor didn't speak to or look at us but lifted up Bella's shirt quickly looking at her bumps. He turned away saying nothing but by his body language I felt he wasn't immediately ready to give her clearance. A feeling of dread came over me as I thought internally this wasn't going to be as easy as our guide predicted.

Once upstairs we were seen by one of the original two doctors we'd seen on Saturday. He asked if we'd put the cream on twice a day as he'd prescribed. We lied and said yes. Bella's bumps were not gone which puzzled him and again they looked bad. They were blotchy and I tried to explain they looked worse when she was hot. We were then seen by another doctor and eventually five doctors came, looked at Bella and stood talking to each other and our guide in Chinese.

Rob was seated holding Bella and I stood watching the doctors. They were discussing Bella while shaking their heads not looking directly at us. They asked us no questions and it was my impression we were not to speak. We had no voice in the matter and might as well have been invisible as far as they were concerned.

Internally I was on the verge of a meltdown and in my thoughts I was screaming at myself to hold it together. All I wanted to do was cry and beg them to release Bella so we could go home on time. I could not understand why they were making this so difficult. Bella had dermatology issues and this was her documented reason for being in the special needs program. Her skin was not going to look good until we could get her the proper lotions. But I kept hearing from deep within to "have patience" and keep my emotions in check. Then one by one the doctors walked away until we were alone in the hallway.

The implications of all the doctors walking away left a lot up in the air. We didn't have one doctor who would take ownership of our case. When they all walked away to deal with other patients we had no idea if any of them would come back to us or not. Any delay would cause us to miss our Visa appointment for Bella which was necessary for us to leave the country. Our guide said the problem was none of the doctors could agree on whether Bella had scabies or chicken pox. He said a diagnosis of scabies would not keep us from getting our medical clearance or getting back into the States but chicken pox would.

I took a long look at our guide and knew he would do the best he could for us. He had a very strong personality and was deeply committed to place Chinese orphans in the hands of good families. But he was not God and would be able to go no further than what God would divinely give him ability to do. In other words, he would not be able to use his own strength and ability to circumvent what God wanted to emerge from this. Whether he knew it or not he was part of the divine plan for us unfolding moment by moment.

Right then, I began to have a strange feeling while Time was ticking as usual I was allowed to operate on another level in slow motion. During what we know as seconds of earthly time I had the ability to have long periods of eternal time to think about things. I reflected on myself and held a very deep knowledge I was made of dust. An intricately woven pile of dust no doubt but ultimately just one piece of tiny dust among millions of other tiny pieces of dust. I felt small and insignificant compared to the vast universe.

As dust, I had no control over the outcome of today's events and had absolutely nothing of value to offer which would make a difference. I could not use tears to sway the doctors. I had no position, authority, influence or money. I was completely helpless and knew if God didn't act on our behalf in some mighty way we would not receive clearance to leave the country on time. I remember simply telling God, "If I ever needed You – <u>it's now</u>"!

Unexpectedly, I heard another series of taunts from our unseen enemy which made the hair stand up on the back of my neck. He screamed very forcefully, "You have no power here. Your faith won't work. God can't hear you. He can't hear your prayers because I (satanic forces) control the airspace above you. God will not come through for you. You have wasted your time serving Him."

When you read those sentences I hope you know they weren't just words on a page to me. I was in a terrible situation and they hit me powerfully. The threats were furiously screeched at me by many voices in unison and a great deal of fear came with them. They were designed to make me feel frail, oppressed and discouraged. What really bugged me about what the demon(s) said was I did <u>feel</u> alone. The airspace around me was silent and felt dead - totally void of life. I did not feel the presence of God and I had not heard the voice of the Holy Spirit as I was accustomed to.

But for some reason this particular spiritual attack made me more mad than afraid. I whispered, "I don't need your airspace to pray or for God to hear me. He can hear me any time and in any place. I have a private prayer language from my spirit to His Spirit." Then I began urgently praying in tongues under my breath.

Rob began talking to a couple from Texas in the hallway who were also waiting for a doctor's medical clearance for their adopted daughter. I smiled when Rob introduced me to them but holding Bella I continued to pace and pray. I was serious about what I was doing and was not going to get caught up in small talk and miss our miracle. I was interrupted by a nurse who rushed us into an exam room to take Bella's temperature.

It was a perfect 98.6. We went back into the hallway and our guide told us to go to another waiting area some distance from where he and the doctors would be.

We found a space of our own, sort of, but were being watched by about seventy five Chinese people all waiting to have various medical procedures done. Of course we stood out like a sore thumb and felt like our parenting skills were on display. We tried to keep Bella entertained in our arms but she wanted to crawl and explore. We struggled as she touched seats and floors as we kept thinking about the germs she was being exposed to. One young boy near us had to go to the bathroom. Instead of going to the nearby lavatory someone brought over a wastebasket and sat him on it. They didn't wipe the boy or dispose of the bag in the wastebasket.

We kept watching the room where our guide and several doctors would float in and out of expectantly hoping for a quick decision. I was becoming concerned because I had only one diaper left and no milk or food for Bella. There were no clocks in the medical facility. We'd left our computers and cell phones on the bus because these were not allowed in the Embassy. Rob and I looked knowingly at each other sensing we'd been there much longer than ten minutes and missed our visa appointment.

Things looked pretty bad for us at that moment. Sometimes circumstances look bad so we'll come to the conclusion there is no hope in ourselves or others. We must look to God for deliverance.

Even if you are in a situation which looks and feels hopeless I would encourage you to never give up on God. Admit your helplessness and watch Him turn it into hopefulness by the strength of His Spirit.

LIGHT FROM A DARK NIGHT

11 The Test of Separation

I continued to pray in tongues under my breath and felt an increasing separation from our situation. I was present physically because I was interacting with everything happening including talking to Rob and taking care of Bella. But I had a strong sense I was watching all of this happen as if I was detached from myself and watching a scene play out in a movie.

I wasn't following a script but it seemed like it. Somehow I had everything I needed in perfect timing. I surprised myself by how deeply peaceful I could act while my mind was stressed out because I didn't know what was going to happen next. It felt like I was two people at the same time. One part of me (my spirit) completely trusted God and had faith to patiently wait for him to act on our behalf.

The other part of me (my flesh) wanted to cry and throw a two year old tantrum. Even at my age, yelling was the only answer my flesh had to overcome the feeling of being helpless and out of control. Acting out in frustration may work sometimes to get our own way but not when we're in a test about our ability to walk by the Spirit and not by flesh.

How do we know we walk according to the Spirit and not the flesh? When our spirit by God's Spirit can override something we deeply want to do which stands opposed to God's will for our life. Galatians 5:16-17 says:

- ❖ "But I say, walk *and* live [habitually] in the [Holy] Spirit [responsive to *and* controlled *and* guided by the Spirit]; then you will certainly not gratify the cravings *and* desires of the flesh (of human nature without God). For the desires of the flesh are opposed to the [Holy] Spirit, and the [desires of the] Spirit are opposed to the flesh (godless human nature); for these are antagonistic to each other [continually withstanding and in conflict with each other], so that you are not free *but* are prevented from doing what you desire to do."

Paul clearly explains why we have inner conflict while trying to live a life of faith. Our flesh and spirit are constantly at war fighting for control. If you have the desire to do something good like control your emotions but cannot, maybe your flesh is ruling your spirit. Your fleshly soul is keeping you from doing those good things you desire to do.

The highest level of our tri-part being is our spirit. It is the place governed by the Holy Spirit and hears, follows and possesses the power to overcome Self (which resides in the soul) to complete life assignments ordained by God. The key is choosing to follow your spirit not your flesh by being trained through the many trials of life until your spirit becomes dominant.

Being in situations where you are out of (self) control will help you know whether you are truly trusting God with your life or not. If you are always in control; able to conquer every situation with your own ability or known faith then you have left no room to test your strength in Christ. On the other hand allowing yourself to be out of control (relinquishing the right to go your own way) for the sake of Christ will bear the good fruit you desire.

When we release control into the hands of Christ we can be sure He will lead us in a kind way. He is not just a shepherd. He is *The Good* Shepherd.   Meditating on different aspects of what a shepherd does for his flock may help us trust Christ more. The shepherd doesn't drive his flock harshly and neither does Jesus. As the Shepard of our life Jesus is kind, loving and protective. And as God, He is Good. He loves you and you could not choose a better route than the way he is already preparing ahead of you. With God leading you- your path is an already God walked path.   This is how we are to live and it's the reason we have everything we need already available at just the right time.

God has given us some mighty weapons to pull down strongholds overcoming evil with good. Strongholds can be internal or external. They are fortified areas of our own mind or world belief systems standing against God which we've agreed with. When I looked at myself in humility understanding my place as one made of dust I was given a sharpened weapon of patience to use for this particular battle.

Patience is defined as: the capacity to accept or tolerate delay, trouble, or suffering without getting angry or upset. This doesn't seem like a mighty weapon so why would God give me patience? Because I was wrestling with spiritual powers and therefore was given a spiritual weapon! I needed a weapon to overcome a spiritual attack not a physical one. I would have looked for a gun or knife even words to overcome a human attack but patience can be used to win without any of these against a spiritual foe.

Patience is a mighty weapon because it shows a great deal of self-control and a deference of power to God overcoming fortified belief systems. One such belief system confronted me saying, "I am being treated unfairly. I have a right to be upset at the doctors and adoptive system (place your own situation into this sentence) therefore I should offload this burden by making someone else pay." Christianity as presented by Christ stands opposed to this belief system. Being treated unfairly is an opportunity to keep our mouth shut and operate on a higher plane, a higher law, with expectancy for God's intervention on our behalf. The higher law is of course, love which bears all things.[xxiv]

Patience was also needed to trust God's timing and ways were worth denying my Self for. When waiting on God we are not to be careless or mindless but are to be sober, vigilant, and watchful. In so doing, our spiritual sight will become more focused. With this particular type of sight we wait before acting and watch for a sign from the spiritual realm for guidance.

The guidance I heard from deep within was, "Be patient. Give God room to work. Watch for Him". While I already had patience in my spirit, I never needed to use it in this mighty way before. It welled up from within and all I had to do was yield to it. [xxv]

Of course patience seemed ridiculous to my fleshly self and thoughts of demanding answers and yelling kept trying to creep out of me. But my spirit was stronger and overrode those impulses. Patience in particular is associated with trials as we read in James 1:2-4 (THE MESSAGE):

"Consider it a sheer gift, friends, when tests and challenges come at you from all sides. You know that under pressure, your faith-life is forced into the open and shows its true colors. So don't try to get out of anything prematurely. Let it do its work so you become mature and well-developed, not deficient in any way."[xxvi]

Patience, endurance and steadfastness are <u>brought out</u> by a trial or temptation designed to prove or test the quality of your faith. These are powerful <u>fruits</u> of faith. They are the after effects from your labor of love and obedience to Christ. They cannot be owned externally by hanging a Scripture verse on a wall. Wearing a necklace which says, "Patience" for instance is a nice reminder of what we want to do. Reminders are good and have their place but we are looking for possession of them.

The fruit of patience, endurance, and steadfastness are brought forth internally as fruit of the Holy Spirit. They are gifts already proven by Christ for you to open, own and use experientially. Only after using them in a test and winning the victory do you own them. Once owned continue to use them as powerful weapons against enemies in the spiritual realm.

Remember, <u>patience must mix with faith</u>[xxvii] to inherit God's promises and its patience which carries the assurance of being developed fully and lacking nothing. Through patience you have the opportunity to become perfect. Being made perfect through patience is not prideful so as to say you'll never make a mistake again. It's stating by mastering patience you must use and be developed by so many other spiritual gifts therefore by and through the process you've been perfected.

As we were in the waiting room I reflected on what was happening and reasoned quickly I was really being presented with tests of separation. Tests of separation are very serious because you must choose a side like when you chose to move from darkness to light; from the devil to God. So is a test of separation to move from self (soul) to spirit. There is absolutely no middle ground to stand on.

According to the Bible, the Word who is Christ can divide the soul from the spirit.[xxviii] So in this test, you must choose Christ. Maybe you think you've already chosen Christ through salvation and this seems like nonsense to choose him again. But I assure you – it's not nonsense! Upon salvation you did choose Christ but it takes time to cleanse your mind and spirit from the filth of the world and its ideas and ways. You must learn to do much over again like a baby such as being able to discern where thoughts and urges come from- soul or spirit.

None of this is new really. I'm just restating activity of our tri-part being in a way you'd understand. The apostles wrote about God's Kingdom and the opposition to it. They outlined worldly thoughts and ways such as bitterness and strife as being opposed to godly ways such as love and peace. They told us to choose our path following Christ and not stray from it.

Well, upon choosing Christ and being washed with the water of the Word, your spirit begins being fed by the living waters- and becomes stronger and stronger. Your spirit is hearing from God and operating on levels you may be unaware of. At some point your spirit wants to take the lead. At about the same time your soul is awakened to the idea it can no longer lead you where God wants you to go. The human soul cannot hear from God except through the spirit and becomes aware it does not have the capacity to lead.

Yet the soul does not give up easily. But because Christ has divided the two, we have become consciously aware of the split and must choose one or the other to lead. I cannot say these tests are ever easy because we always feel like we're denying our very self. And truly we are but only of what is not necessary for our purpose. This is why Peter says the "goal of faith is the saving of our soul". I always thought he was talking about salvation upon death but the saving of our soul is very important and happens while on earth. A regenerated soul who defers to a born again spirit will now be able to receive and process messages from God correctly.

The job of separating is a work you will do with the guidance of the Holy Spirit and the power of Jesus Christ. Only He has the power and knowledge to divide the soul and spirit who are so closely knit together. So in this test, to have victory, you have to decide to go all in and make the switch to rule your life from your spirit and not your Self.

On another front, aside from this internal battle, the screeching statements made by my unseen enemy were clearly designed to destroy my faith. Through one avenue or another I felt like Satan desired to wipe me out completely. And so this test of separation was of the highest order and would determine if I was going to remain a God follower after this or if I was going to follow the way of Satan. There is no neutral ground and this test separates nominal Christians from those who desire to be powerful sons of God.

Again, you might have some questions as to where I'm going with this. Don't all Christians follow God? How is it possible for a Christian to follow Satan? Whether you know it or not you are either a Christ follower or a self- follower. Being a follower of Self stands opposed to Christ who did not follow his own self-will but did the will of the Father God. So Christians who choose to follow the god of themselves are really still following <u>the ways of</u> the god of this world.

We don't belong to Satan anymore and are not left alone to reject his ways. Now we have God on our side who will help us overcome. But many, think following Christ after salvation is automatic! They don't invest in their spiritual life at all – and may think this is the job of their pastor. But it takes work – spiritual work – to bring about the kind of change needed to actually be about denying self and doing the will of the Father.

It takes more than lip service to prove whose path you are chasing after. It takes a test of separation! Don't worry about being presented with the "test of your life" unprepared. The

Holy Spirit will guide, prepare and lead you through a series of tests and trials. I can say pretty strongly though, our enemy always thinks we will fail and revels in bringing a child of God down. But God is not like that. He works in us. He knows when the timing is right and when we have had enough spiritual training to enter in a contest such as this. Yet, our will is our will. He never takes this away from us and the reason this is a contest with a real win or lose scenario is because the choice to move deeper into him or away from him is ours to make.

For this reason, you will not be able to turn away from God in this test and go back to Him easily with the same strength of character. Think of it in natural terms such as with a man and a woman. A certain man tells a woman he loves her. She believes him and in fact has no reason to doubt what he says. But then a test comes along. Maybe he accepts a job in another city without consulting her and she believes he's chosen money over her. Or maybe he accepts a dinner invitation from a female co-worker of hers causing her to doubt his motivation. Whatever the case may be a breach in trust has occurred. She may decide to end all contact with this man. Or she may allow him back into her life with reservations. God has higher ways than we do so I'm careful not to say he would turn totally away from us. However, He is jealous for us and I believe if we turn away in a test of separation we will need to go back and repair the breach in trust before we can move forward again.

I chose to believe in God and to know nothing but Him. This might seem like an easy decision but at the time it took great strength to push through intense pressure and fear mounted against me to deny Christ. With my decision made, I could go on the offensive over the statements made against me and God by the unseen spiritual enemy.

The first lie the enemy wanted me to believe was I was alone and, "God could not hear me". I did feel alone. I cannot say I didn't. I felt like I just couldn't connect with God the way in which I was used to. The closest I can get to describing how I felt would be as a student feels while taking a test at school. The teacher is present in the room but has done their teaching and is now silent on the subject matter. It's time for the student to prove she knows the material. It's a test of separation from learner to owner.

It's funny, as I think of things in the context of a test at school, this wasn't an open book test either! I did not have my Bible with all my underlines and notes. I had no means to look up Scripture on the internet. No cheat sheets. I could not have quoted the exact book and verse then like I am in this book. I simply had to know my material: "Nothing can separate me from the love of Christ not even a demon".[xxix] Therefore, since God could hear me at home he must be able to hear me now. Unlike a mute Buddha or dead Confucius who had shrines dedicated to them all around us in China -our God is the only true <u>Living</u> God who hears and responds.

However, there is precedence for satanic forces to block airspace in the book of Daniel. The Satanic enemy withstood and held an angel sent to deliver Daniel an answer to his prayer for twenty one days. When the angel finally met Daniel he told him not to be afraid because his words were heard.[xxx] We shouldn't be afraid and think God does not hear us. He hears our prayers and inquiries from the moment we "set our minds to understand and humble ourselves before God".[xxxi]

The enemy said, "God could not <u>hear</u> me because satanic forces were blocking the airspace." Let's learn from Daniel: our prayers are <u>heard</u> the moment we release them but it can be <u>our answer</u> which is blocked or delayed. The enemy wanted me to believe my prayers weren't heard so any delay in my answer would be cause to lose faith.

God can answer our prayers in many ways. Sometimes answers come directly from the Word of God and other times the Holy Spirit might use someone to deliver it. If you set your mind to understand something and have humbled yourself before God expect an answer in whatever form he sends it. You must not give up no matter how long it takes.

If angels can be hindered by satanic forces it stands to reason a human vessel carrying a word from God might also be delayed for various reasons. Think of a time you were stirred to call a friend with encouragement or give someone something and didn't do it. Your faith was ready to move but you were busy or reasoned yourself right out of it. Or maybe you've been the person praying for help but did not follow an urge to be somewhere at a certain time where someone was waiting to deliver an answer. There can be other ways we are hindered from receiving answer to our prayers but it's important for us who have the Holy Spirit to follow his lead and act when it is our time to act knowing we will be used give and receive help.

Having settled God could hear me meant He was aware of what was happening to me. The next screeching lie from the enemy to be dealt with was: by controlling the airspace he (satanic forces) had control of the situation. And most probably he did! But while they may have been able to control the situation- <u>they did not have control over the outcome!</u>

I chose to pray in tongues with my secret prayer language simply because it came naturally. I didn't have to think about it I just knew I did not need the physical airspace above me and beneath God where the spirits move because God's Spirit lives in me.[xxxii] I don't have to go any further than to delve within tapping in to the living waters flowing inside to be in touch with God-thanks be to Jesus Christ![xxxiii]

As Christians we know but must individually own: God came in bodily form in the person of Christ to live, die and rise to eternal life in order to dwell with and in man. Christ is Emanuel; God with us. Christ said it was better for him to leave the world so the Holy Spirit could come. He as man could only touch so many but God's Omnipotence through the Holy Spirit's presence can be with all of us -always.

We must hold strong to this truth: God lives in us. Then we won't be tossed about in our belief system every time we encounter external pressures and problems. We will also experience firsthand one of the greatest mysteries of our faith which is: Christ in us is our hope of glory.[xxxiv]

I also prayed in tongues to birth a spiritual answer for my situation because "What is born of (from) the flesh is flesh (of the physical is physical); and what is born of the Spirit is spirit."[xxxv] There was nothing my flesh could birth in this situation except to destroy the work of God about to manifest. I truly needed an answer born from above not able to be hindered by myself or any enemy of God.

When praying in tongues we speak to God directly, "For one who speaks in an [unknown] tongue <u>speaks not to men but to God</u>, for no one understands or catches his meaning, because <u>in the</u> [Holy] Spirit he utters secret truths *and* hidden things [not obvious to the understanding]."[xxxvi] By praying in tongues we release hidden truth.

The truth isn't hidden from God but from our understanding. When we pray <u>in the</u> Holy Spirit we allow our voice to be used by God to declare those things previously hidden. In other words answers, opportunities, salvation, healing, ways of escape, deliverance, release, forgiveness and an infinite number of other things which are declared by God through you (for you personally or others) in an unknown spiritual language carry power because of the authority God gave mankind to govern the earth.

Don't worry if you can't understand the words the Holy Spirit is praying through you. It doesn't matter! They are heard and understood by God and in the spiritual realm. And God may give another person understanding who can speak the mystery out in your language or He might give you the direct interpretation. Whether it's interpreted at the moment it's spoken doesn't matter either. You might have declared an answer to a problem that has yet to come into existence. In which case you will have the knowledge to know or do something at just the right moment.

Your part in this is to pray what you hear in the language you hear from your spirit. If your mind just can't get past not understanding you can begin by having your Bible handy. Pray in tongues out loud and read the Bible with your mind. Have your mind think on Scripture as you pray. This way you can make your mind fruitful by using it to seek God with language you do know.

Could I have prayed in English and not in tongues at all? Maybe but I'd like you to ponder a few things. One is our capacity to communicate with God and each other on a higher plane. On the day of Pentecost those who were spiritual from different nations and speaking different languages all understood the same message from Peter. Others who were not spiritual thought Peter was drunk and spoke nonsense. How was this possible except by the existence of a divine channel of communication discerned by the spiritual man only? One day tongues whether known or unknown will cease.[xxxvii] Then our spirits in Heaven will communicate in a way we do not know of now.

Secondly, when an individual believer speaks in tongues she is learning to open up a channel of communication between her and God. By speaking words no man can understand she puts her rational thinking down and instead is open to God through the Holy Spirit to pray out mysteries for her own life. I recently read a blog post by Praying Medic. In it he cites a study conducted to monitor the brain of those praying in tongues. They found out what we know: The Holy Spirit prays through us bypassing the part of the brain we would normally use to think and speak. The words we pray are truly not our own but God's.[xxxviii]

Those mysteries we speak are part of the deep things of God and have not been revealed to anyone. They are meant to build up your inner man. Building up your inner man is of great importance. From there, you will have the strength to conquer deep seated strongholds hindering your walk of faith.

Honestly, my story is not about whether speaking in tongues is for today. But to be truly faithful in sharing my life story with you I want to include all which makes me- me. And obtaining our future heavenly inheritance now in this life to whatever degree is possible always exists in Christ. Why would we not explore our treasure chests when given the keys by God?

Even if we disagree on the subject of tongues I'd like to impart what the Holy Spirit once gave me when I was about to discount someone else's faith who emphatically did not believe speaking in tongues (a language not acquired naturally)[xxxix] was for today.

❖ "But I urge *and* entreat you, brethren, by the name of our Lord Jesus Christ, that all of you be in perfect harmony *and* full agreement in what you say, and that there be no dissensions *or* factions *or* divisions among you, but that you be perfectly united in your common understanding and in your opinions *and* judgments."[xl]

After I read this verse the Holy Spirit told me I "could either be part of the problem or the solution. It was my choice." I decided it was more important not to judge another believer over matters of the Holy Spirit but to be in unity and peace with each other thereby proving ourselves to be Christ's followers.[xli] I made the decision to be part of the solution and have been blessed from this person and ministry. I am humble enough to understand the Holy Spirit can work through men in any way He chooses. Let's not allow disagreements arising from our own personal faith preferences or personalities hinder the Spirit of unity we should uphold.

Now I'd like to relay something I have recently begun to delve into. It is about discerning the difference between truth and deception. It's important to understand which one you are dealing with at the onset of a spiritual battle. If you remember from my dark night of the soul I searched for the "element of truth" after each dart the enemy shot my way by reflecting on the statements or screams as they were.

In the case of "what kind of a mother are you – you left your daughter alone", I searched for and found plenty of ways I was not a good mother- <u>truth according to my own standards</u>. Was I really searching for the truth? Yes and No. I thought I was searching for the truth but I didn't go to God first or think about what He would say on my behalf. Instead I searched my mind for confirming experiences or feelings to corroborate or reject what the enemy said. But my mind never rejected the enemy's accusations and never stood up for me – it's very own self. The mind will follow deceptive statements and can come up with situations to back it up and in my case went right to work trying to find the truth while following a deceptive premise which was "I was a bad mother".

Satan and his forces present us with deception to see what we will buy and accept as truth. This is happening more often than we realize. Maybe you aren't attacked over your mothering. Maybe with you it's about self-esteem, pride, job, ability, faith- any area the enemy sees as a sensitive spot. From personal experience: your mind probably will find something from your life to agree with the lies a satanic enemy places before you.

So then, your mind is not the first place you should look for truth or a defending response. I only defeated the enemy when God's truth rose up from within my spirit. I knew and even my mind knew - <u>this</u> truth was real. Buying anything less than God's Truth won't place us closer to Christ but will drive us away with a feeling of condemnation. If you feel condemned maybe for no known reason don't run away from God instead ask for His grace to uncover the truth. Then ask for mercy and forgiveness if needed.

You might wonder what God's truth is. Truth is Christ. Christ is Truth.[xlii] As believers we live <u>in Light</u> and <u>in Truth</u> because we live <u>in Christ</u>. Anything and I repeat anything coming against Truth in our life because we live in God's kingdom is really an <u>element of deception</u>. It is an open trap set to see if we will walk through it or not.

For instance you may have had an enemy send you a deceptive screeching dart like me, "You've wasted your time and served God for nothing." Any one of us could look back over our life and focus on unanswered prayer, disappointments, and so forth and become discouraged. That's Satan's design! He wants us to be discouraged and turn from God so we will not look to him in hope and with expectancy. Satan chooses for us to believe we are no further ahead in life for serving God. But we know from God's word – <u>no one serves God for nothing</u>. He rewards those who diligently seek him here on earth and in the life to come.

It's our choice to live in deception or truth. When I was going through my dark night of the soul the week before, I was afraid and let deceptive words mingle with my thoughts. I lingered over them a little too long letting my feelings get involved. Each time it took me a while to recover the truth. The accusations made in this chapter were of the same type but I started looking at them through faith and answering faster knowing they were false.

Being able to discern deception is very important for the believer. Even if we are living in the light we can still be deceived on various fronts. If we don't catch the deception early we might walk around in the wilderness thinking we are doing things in faith when we are not.

God does exist and He does love you. If He has given you a trial of separation of any kind to prove your faith or your love for him there is nothing nobler you could be doing. Fighting to believe in Him against all odds when you can't see into the heavenly clearly produces a sweet fragrance pleasing to the Father.

It is because of our love for God we hope in what we cannot see. There is coming a time when everyone will see Christ in all His majesty clearly. Then, every knee will bend before Him not just those who worshipped him on earth. When this happens the time for proving our love is over and our eternity has already been set.

Everything you do physically and spiritually is moving you toward a great moment. Spend your time wisely praying and preparing in the presence of Christ. Your power, authority, and victory as a believer depends on it.

LIGHT FROM A DARK NIGHT

12 Heaven Opens Up

We were still waiting for a decision from the doctors' on whether they would release Bella or not. My spiritual enemy was doing everything to get me to deny my faith and disown the existence of the God of the Bible. Attacks kept flowing like, "There is no God (the implication being there is a god but not the God I believe in). God doesn't love you. Who is God? Where is your God? You are not going to hear from Him. You are not important. Who are you to Him?"

I continued to pray in tongues and quarreled with those statements internally. The pressure was so great to deny the existence of God and at one point I remember almost feeling like I could go insane. I wondered if I wasn't the crazy one to believe in a God I'd never seen. What if everything was a lie and the life of faith I knew was just a concoction of my mind? I thought about the possibility there was no God and let my mind carry out every one of its thoughts to the farthest extreme it could go. At the conclusion of it all my mind fully conceded to this belief: if my God, the Living God I knew and believed in did not exist then neither did I and all life would be utterly pointless and void of purpose.

In the midst of this fierce spiritual struggle I opened up a new stream of thought and began focusing on God's promise to make himself real to me.[xliii] Retreating into my own thoughts of Jesus seemed to silence all the enemy was doing or maybe he was still working but I ceased to care. All I could do was think about how much I loved Jesus. Desperately I longed to know if He loved me too. You might wonder how I could not know his love for me was real. After all He died on a cross for me and my sins and if I was a woman of faith surely this would be the basis of it. And of course it is!

But I wasn't longing to reach back to the beginning of my saving faith – I was longing to be <u>known as His</u>- as his bride. I wanted to experience the feeling of being part of the bride of Christ. To be known as a spiritual spouse of Christ. I was looking for Him to show himself strong on my behalf just as a husband would defend his wife who was being confronted with evil. How did I get to the place where I would even require to know God's love in this way?

Jesus had become as necessary to me as my own breath. If I had an obsession it had been to know Him more. A few months before being in China we were vacationing on Hilton Head Island, South Carolina. I had a rare opportunity to sit on the beach alone with my dad one late afternoon. We both clutched a book and sunk our beach chairs in the sand. The waves lapped up to us every so often and this was and still is my idea of heaven on Earth! We talked a little bit about God and faith. At one point I looked out into the horizon and said within myself, "I don't care what anyone else chooses to believe or do, I'm going to spend the rest of my life getting to know Christ more".

This statement birthed my special quest and over the course of the next few months I prayed and read my Bible with renewed purpose. The Holy Spirit led me to several new (to me) authors many of whom lived 100 to 300 years before. They were great men, A.B. Simpson, Matthew Henry, Andrew Murray and Charles Finney. I felt a comradery with their writings and connected to their spiritual journeys.

At some point all of us should reach back in time with one hand touching the faith that was and let it work through us while reaching out the other hand to touch the faith of the future. The faith of the past is in our spiritual genealogy. We should research our fathers and mothers in the faith to better understand ourselves paying close attention when feeling a deep connection to their life or writings. In some way, their faith and what they came to know of Christ, is available to us like an already opened stream of faith. We can begin where they left off adding our faith on top of theirs. Advancement will come much quicker this way.

I also found some contemporary authors like Rick Joyner and Ana Mendez Ferrell who opened my eyes to see the current stream of faith and where it is leading all of us who wind up on this mission. What was my pursuit? To seek God simply for the purpose of knowing Him. I didn't want anything from God. Of course I still had needs and prayer requests. But during this time greater than any need I had was the necessity to know God and be known by him. This pathway led to some beautiful revelation into His Word as never before.

After such closeness with God can you imagine how lonely I felt pacing the floor of a Chinese Hospital not feeling Him near me like I was used to? I needed God. I needed His person badly and couldn't figure out why this moment was so different than any other time in my life. Why did I need Him now like never before? It's not like I'd never prayed an urgent or important prayer before. But why did the heavens seem shut to me? Why was God silent and why couldn't I hear His voice? Last chapter I wrote about the test of separation. But this was hindsight for in the moment I had no idea what was happening to me or why.

Fear was trying to overcome and tempt me to think God would not come through for me. Fear laid a trap saying God was not real and for this reason I would get no response. Fear said God did not care about me. Fear said I was nobody to Him. But in spite of fear and my circumstances I did not give up. I pushed and pulled on God more and was resolute in one thing: I was not leaving this space without seeing God manifest Himself to me in some way.

Suddenly, faster than the blink of an eye, I was not in a Chinese hospital anymore. My body was but my spirit had been thrust into a different place and I began to tremble. The atmosphere was nothing like that of earth. The air (if it was air) is thicker, heavier. I knew I was in the presence of God as would anyone whether they believe in him on earth or not. I stood alone and everything was dark around me. It was not an evil darkness because I felt no fear. It was just darkness as if I alone had been singled out and stood on display. Think of it like being a lone performer on a dark stage and the only visible light comes from one spotlight focused solely on you. I felt like I was waiting for an entrance into the next place and heard nothing except my own thoughts which seemed to drift upward as I thought them.

I shook as I felt my spirit bow low in deep humility before the Creator. There could be no doubt I was created from dust. In this solitary dark space I sobbed and was very upset because I did not have a gift to bring before God. The song sung at Christmas called "The little drummer boy", kept ringing through my head: "I have no gift to bring Pa Rum Pum Pum Pum". I knew I had nothing of value to bring the Great King but my mind kept trying to find some gift of worth to lay before God. Finally I gave up. No gift seemed worthy or appropriate. Quivering, not knowing what would happen to me since I had no gift, I said, "Lord, I have no gift to bring you. I have only myself".

He answered, "Your self is enough". Out of the darkness a golden scepter was extended toward me. I took the end of it and entered the next room. I walked up to a bar (like a railing) and stood there. Looking around everything I could see was in various shades of the color gray. Through a veil like screen I could make out two silhouettes. One figure was seated on what appeared to be a judge's bench. The bench sat up high, was huge and imposing. I knew this bench or throne was for God the Father.

The other silhouette was seated a little ways from me before the Judge. His posture was conversational like a son talking to his dad about a serious matter. I felt loved by Him and knew this was Jesus. They seemed to have been in discussion about me. I saw no one else except one to my left who smiled throughout the proceeding. However I sensed there were others in the room. There was an electricity present like in a courtroom hushed with expectancy waiting for the secret star witness to come forth.

Slowly and purposefully the voice of the Father said, "What.... Do.... You... Want...?" Each word sounded like thunder and carried power that rippled out into the universe. Knowing I could have whatever I asked for I responded with boldness, "I ask for all the angels you would release to my command to do what I cannot. I ask that they move on the one doctor who would be the most inclined to listen to the Spirit of God. All we need is one doctor to release Bella."

As soon as I spoke my request, a gavel brought down a curtain and my vision ended abruptly. I continued to pray knowing I had been granted what was asked for: Bella's release. Angels were dispatched to work on our behalf. Soon our guide appeared outside of the room where he and the doctors had been. He waved his hands for us to follow him and we started walking quickly to exit the building. He had our clearance papers in a sealed envelope and was not waiting around for anyone to change their mind.

Our guide explained Bella's orphanage faxed documentation showing Bella had chicken pox when she was four months old. This was news to us as we were not given any medical history for her time spent in the orphanage. Our guide said this was very unusual for the orphanage to give out this documentation. He felt it was because the adoption agency had such a good relationship with the orphanage. Even if that were the case it was still God at work in advance of our visit seeing to it we would have what we needed at exactly the right time. But I still believe to this day the credit for Bella's release belongs to God. It was His angels at work moving on our behalf doing what we could not. And in the end it was one doctor who signed the medical clearance for Bella- the one we'd met on the elevator.

I was overwhelmed by what I had seen in the vision but didn't have time to think about any of it. We were rushing downstairs and across the street to the American Embassy to pick up the other families in our group. While we missed our original appointment our guide was able to get us another time slot later in the day. Rob and I were disappointed we could not tie up this one last loose end. Our exit out of China was contingent upon getting this visa and we would not be settled until it was in our hands.

Our bus was parked some distance from the American Embassy per regulation. I was concerned Bella would melt down for lack of milk and food if we didn't get my bag on the bus soon. There were hundreds of people walking around and I didn't want them to think I could not take care of Bella.

The scene outside of the American Embassy was full of high energy. The sidewalks out front were teeming with people and hundreds formed an orderly line to get in. I thought if we had to stand in that line we'd never get in for our appointment today. Everyone stared at us which by now we had become accustomed to. The older women smiled at Bella. Our guide ran into a friend and was in conversation with him while we stood casually taking in the scene.

Our guide received a phone call and began to shout at us to follow him. He began running and to keep up with him I was bumping in to people. I didn't want to hurt Bella or appear rude so I grabbed onto his shirt and yelled at Rob to keep up. We had no idea what was happening but knew it was urgent.

We bypassed the long waiting line and went to another doorway in the back of the building. Our guide started yelling at the guard who was giving a deaf ear to an American service man pleading to get into the Embassy with his Chinese wife. Again I didn't want to be rude to the serviceman and cut in front of him but our guide ripped the guard's clipboard out of his hand and started flipping pages. He kept yelling our names and the adoption agency while pointing his fingers at the papers. We were indeed on the list and showed our passports to the guard. Our guide shoved us inside. Due to some recent rule changes he was not allowed to go in with us.

Once inside I felt instant calm and peace because it was so quiet. We were body scanned and moved forward past the guards. We stood there not knowing what to do next. Our guide cracked the door and yelled we could still make our appointment. He told us to go through the door and run.

We went through the door which led outside and found ourselves in a large courtyard. There were no signs pointing us in the right direction. Somehow we knew to run straight, then right and left turning a corner. A sign written in English said, "Adoption" with an arrow pointing toward another door. We rushed inside and again it was peaceful and really beautiful. The space was all glass and metal with hundreds waiting their turn to gain a visa.

We were about to take the elevator upstairs when a guard appeared out of nowhere. He smiled and said the stairs were faster. At the top of the stairs we saw our friends. They told us to get a numbered ticket and we sat down for a minute catching up with everyone.

Our number was called and we stepped up to the counter. It was similar to a bank teller window with a thick glass partition separating us from the workers. We passed our papers under a slot at the bottom of the glass and stood nervously. Some of these documents had been filled out months ago and my insides were in turmoil hoping I'd filled out everything properly.

I was teary eyed at the window as an American was helping us. He spoke in English which was comforting to me. After a few minutes at this first window we were asked to go to the next window. Once there another American led us through the swearing in ceremony declarations we'd missed earlier. We then moved back to the first window and were given what we needed. Our guide could pick up Bella's exit visa later that afternoon!

Without God there was no way we would have passed the medicals and made our appointment. I will never forget how

God chose to show Himself to me by opening up a window into Heaven and making so many Scriptures come alive.

Because of what I saw in the vision I know Heaven is attentive to you and your prayers. What happens to you is important. Angels stand ready to move on your behalf at the command of God and as you become a vessel to rule they will move at your command! The Father is truly Lord and Ruler of All. Jesus our precious Savior loves you more than you can fathom. He really is living and making intercession for you before the Father. And the Holy Spirit is with you at all times preparing and empowering you to endure, have patience and be steadfast in your purpose to know and experience the love of the One, True and Holy God. Amen!

LIGHT FROM A DARK NIGHT

LIGHT FROM A DARK NIGHT

13 Seeing into Heaven

As you know, we did make it home from China and on time! Since then, through writing to you I've spent a lot of time reflecting on the vision of Heaven which opened up to me. Seeing into Heaven absolutely changed my life – my thoughts, my perception of reality, and my understanding of God's Word. It seems like God is increasing the prophetic sight of many and when looked at as a collective whole we should begin to develop a picture of the spiritual realm which has largely been unknown territory for the masses in the Church. But even as prophetic voices and Godly visions are coming forth they can be easily dismissed by those who do not yet understand our tri-part being and our ability to operate upon earth and in Heaven through our spirit.

Before looking a little deeper into my vision I feel we should look at visions in general. My purpose here is to give you a basic understanding of visions, how they are possible, why they are given then add layers of understanding upon the vision of Heaven which I was given.

To begin, I was in the spirit when Heaven opened up to me since my body never left the hospital. I can be sure of this since my husband could witness I was present and interfacing with him. Therefore, I was having an open vision because I was awake at the time not asleep or in a trance.

We can experience being fully functional in our body while feeling disconnected to ourselves (as if we were watching ourselves in a movie) because we are a spirit who lives in a body. We have the ability to exist in the realms of the physical and spiritual at the same time and this is how I was able to operate and function in two dimensions at once.

How wonderful we have been made by God who gave us a body to live on earth, a spirit to live in Heaven (or Hell, but that is our choice not God's design) and a soul to be the interface between the two. The soul uses the senses of the body to identify what happens around it and also interprets information from the spirit which is awake to the activity of the spiritual realm around you.

The soul is capable of receiving information to process from both the physical and spiritual world at the same time! However, the soul processes information from the senses most of the time at a higher rate because we have been trained from youth to use, interpret meaning and understand the five senses. We have had little or no training on how to hear, process and understand messages from our spirit or the spiritual dimension. Therefore the mind can make no sense of spiritual information it receives from the soul and dismisses it as imagination.

How do you know if what you are seeing is from God or not? First of all, Jesus told a man he had to be born again to see the Kingdom of God.[xliv] If you are born again you have been granted the gift to see into Heaven and God's Kingdom.

Those who are not born again may see into the spiritual realm but not into the Kingdom of Heaven.

Godly visions are given for various reasons. They move faith forward, answer questions, and give us a picture of coming events. They can change our thinking and birth a new move of the Holy Spirit. Visions also convince us of the realness of Heaven, other dimensions and make the Scriptures come alive. They will always bear Godly fruit leading us and others toward Christ and His image.

The Apostle John tells us to test the spirits to see if Christ would be magnified by them or not.[xlv] So by all means test the vision! Those who receive Godly visions should be moving more toward Christ and His image than the image of Satan and the world. Godly visions and dreams will produce Godly fruit and demonic dreams and visions will produce demonic fruit.

There is nothing wrong with testing prophecy and prophetic vision to a point. Paul tells us to test and prove what is spoken prophetically <u>until we know what is good</u>.[xlvi] In other words, we develop our spirit to recognize truth and what is good by testing and proving prophecy. Until we know and can recognize truth we are not to depreciate or devalue the prophetic. In the last year, I've read books from authors who have advanced their sight into the Kingdom to such a degree its way beyond my understanding. My job is to test and prove what they say while not criticizing because the potential exists for me to grow my spirit and advance into increasing levels of glory in Christ.

If there is no prophetic sight – no peering into the unseen Kingdom of God – then where do we go? Nowhere! And this is precisely why the kingdom of darkness fights the prophetic. The devil doesn't want us to behold Christ or see His Kingdom. He doesn't want us to change from darkness to light or be formed into the image of Christ. The devil would rather we remain bound by religion and religious systems (the formality of them) thus denying the power of the Spirit. He knows how much we don't like change and would rather lead a boring Christian life than go "off the deep end" into a joyous life of liberty in the Spirit.

But seeing Christ in His glory is our blessed heritage! You and I along with all the saints who truly believe in Christ have been given to him as a gift. The Father God gave us to Christ. We belong to Him. We are His Christmas morning – presents laid before Him. And Jesus prayed asking the Father for us to be <u>in Him</u>; to be <u>with Him</u> where He is so we may <u>see</u> His glory![xlvii]

It's true we are seated in Heavenly places which designates our position and authority in Christ but while there our spirit is seeing and participating in Heaven so we can bring what we see to the Earth. As born again believers we actually have access to the Kingdom of God and can transmit God's way of doing things to the mind from our spirit and through the soul. It's an amazing privilege; an amazing prize for which we reach upwards to grasp.

With all this in mind what would God want communicated through me to you? There are four things from my vision important for all of us to know.

- The atmospheric difference between Earth and Spiritual Realm
- The Court of Heaven specifically The Throne of Grace
- The feeling of being "at home" in Heaven
- The Realness of Heaven: Aware and Ready

In one instant I was able to see with my physical eyes alone and then suddenly I was in another dimension able to discern the spiritual realm with no sense of the earthly. The atmosphere was thicker in some way. Heavier might be a better word because I had absolutely no doubt I was in the presence of God. I'm not saying being on Earth we are not in God's presence (being seen by Him at all times) but we don't consciously feel it at all times. We can go about our daily business unaware of God's presence.

Not so in this space. Every shred of it is drenched with the knowledge of God. There is no time or awareness of earthly time. We have no needs and are not aware of what presses us on earth. I cannot stress this point enough- in this space there is no doubt of whether God exists because here He is completely known. It is a place where no devil can hinder our knowledge of God and his existence. God can completely be felt without hindrance.

I know I trembled in this place because of the weight of where I was. If a person were to reach this place through death their eternity would already be set. If they never believed there was a God or refused to trust Jesus Christ while on earth they'd be completely proved wrong because once in this space where the soul has no outward hindrance they'd have no doubt of whether God was for real. You don't want to get to this place without the Salvation of Christ!

As I stood alone in the darkness I knew I wasn't dead and was not in outer space. I had a sensation of being exposed (nothing was hidden) but not in a fearful way. I knew myself to be myself but had no tie to earthly problems, fear, worry, needs - nothing. I never thought about my life, family or anything about anything connected to earth. In fact, I didn't even have a consciousness of earth. It just did not exist in this place.

I was simply alone in this darkness with no one but myself and my own thoughts. As I thought – my thoughts rose upward. My thoughts were not secret or private as they are on earth but they were known as if I'd spoken them aloud. And what was I thinking at a time like this? I was agonizing over not having a gift to bring before the Lord. Somehow I knew I was in waiting and would appear before the Lord. And then what would I present to Him? What could I give to Him- what could I lay at His feet? Not money – it had no place here. Not a prayer – it was not needed here. Not a service I'd performed – it was not appropriate.

I came to the conclusion nothing with earthly value is worthy of God. Until my mind finally gave in I could not come to the place of total acceptance of God's Word: I am saved by Grace and it was not of my own doing but God's gift to me. God is the Giver of gifts and I was going to be allowed to approach Him because of Grace. Not because I had done something to deserve it or had brought the right gift. We cannot do anything to earn seeing into God's Kingdom nor can we buy our way into it. Sight or visions are given by God at his discretion leading us to a deeper love, Christlikeness and to help others.

The instant I admitted to not having a gift other than myself in Christ, I was admitted to the Throne of Grace via the golden scepter. What could the golden scepter be a picture of? When the scepter is held by a king and extended out to one of his subjects it is the offer of pardon, grace, acceptance, access and approachability. When extended toward a "commoner" he or she could approach the king without fear. And according to Matthew Henry(whose commentary is my favorite), it is an offer which Christ holds out extended toward every human being, "Come to Me...".["xlviii"] Christs stands ready to accept with grace, pardon sins, and grant access to the Father for every person who will but receive.

It's to Christ everyone should run to but because of sin we may be afraid to approach the King of All. So he "holds out the golden scepter that we may touch the top of it and may live" by saying the words "...and I will give you rest".[xlix] By giving us a promise of rest not wrath we never need to fear when approaching Him with a need or request.

Having been accepted as being in Christ, I immediately stepped up to the bar of God. My impression was everyone (all of those in Heaven who were witness to the proceedings) saw what was happening to me. I knew The Father and Jesus had been in discussion over me. They weren't wringing their hands wondering what to do but Christ was in the position of interceding for me before the Throne of Grace. What a powerful sight for me to be a witness of and share with you. Christ is praying for you- just like the Bible says!

At the bar (like a railing) I wasn't trembling anymore and felt no anxiety. I did not feel weak but full of youthful, robust strength. I felt familiar with my surroundings like I'd been there before and belonged in this place. I did not have to think or use my mind for anything. I just knew what to do and say. I was completely confident I would not be turned away empty handed.

When God asked what I wanted, I did not need to use my mind to think about what was needed. I was there on a mission and simply yet boldly responded like a general who knew what it would take to win a battle. I needed fierce supernatural help because the earthly procedures in place were merely there to disguise the true nature of what was happening in the spiritual realm. The five doctors who could not agree what to diagnose Bella with probably felt under intense pressure not to release her. Undoubtedly they did not even know why they were making it difficult for this one child to exit the country. The enemy does not like children with a generational descent to worship him gaining freedom through adoption. Adoption is more powerful than you might think because Christian parents will aid their child in turning future generations into Christ followers.

You might be wondering why one life matters so much. Why does one orphan girl matter so much the devil would interfere to the point God would summon me to Heaven's Court on her behalf? <u>Because God has the power to turn an orphan into a son and daughter.</u> Every life is God's – from the beginning and in the end. Once mine, Bella would not be an orphan any longer. She is my daughter and I know no difference between her and the daughter born of my body. They are the same. In the same way, we the Gentiles were once orphans outside of the Jewish nation and outside of God's promises. But through Christ we have been made sons and daughters and are now part of the family grafted in alongside the Jews.

I had no thoughts of taking advantage of where I was or of taking my time to look around. Maybe this is why I was shielded from seeing everything around me. If I'd seen the splendor of Heaven and the multitudes attending the proceedings, I might have been distracted from my mission and desired to stay.

I'm not special in the body of Christ, all of us will be comfortable in Heaven because it is our home. We have citizenship there and through Christ, Heaven can be accessed while yet on earth. One day we will be complete and at ease with our surroundings but for now we struggle because of the tension between Heaven and Earth, spirit and flesh. Our discomfort is because of the hope we have of one day being fully comforted. Our spirit knows, hopes and longs for the perfection coming while our flesh is tied to and longs for the things of this world.

Paul told us to keep our minds set on things above and not on earthly things.[1] Heaven is more real and more perfect than anything on earth because it is eternal. To move forward as the body of Christ we need more sight and vision of what is truly real.

And what is truly real is the love of God and the loving kindness he has placed upon the head of every true believer. If there is one thing I'd like you to take away from this chapter it would be this: Jesus Christ wishes to show Himself to you in a very real way. He wants you to experience what you read in your Bible and what you believe and have faith for. My aim in writing is to wake up your spirit so you will diligently prepare yourself and reach for Christ pulling on Him so every dry place will be watered and become refreshed.

# LIGHT FROM A DARK NIGHT

14 From Flesh to Spirit

In a previous chapter I wrote how I felt like two different people while waiting for the medical clearance papers for Bella. My flesh wanted to scream and throw a fit but my spirit was controlled, watchful and patient. When did I come to the point of being led by the Spirit to the extent I could deny my flesh in an intense situation? And more importantly how did it happen?

The Holy Spirit is the only one who knows when we are ready to face anything. On that day and in that moment; I was ready for the specific test of my faith.

What my spirit gained from being tested is the victory over my flesh. A trophy has been set up as a permanent memorial in my soul. Once you taste victory and know its feeling- it's easier to win again. Now when I'm presented with various times to overcome my flesh (putting down what I want to happen and instead choosing Christ) I have a reference point and can recognize what to do quicker.

Letting our spirit operate over our flesh is something we learn to do day by day and even moment by moment. I have in no way attained perfection in this area and every day presents new challenges. I sometimes cry over my failings. I get angry with myself when I don't do what I want to but I don't dwell on my imperfections too long. Instead, my aim is to keep learning and pressing onward.

So how do we really switch from flesh to spirit or make change effectual in our lives? John 3 relates the work of the Holy Spirit to wind. We know the wind is there but can't see where it came from or where it is going. That's why it's hard to give someone a step by step process on how sanctification works. The Holy Spirit comes to you from somewhere in your life to bring healing and wholeness and then takes you in another direction known to only him. Sometimes His work is unseen and undetected by you. In fact, if you trust Him and cooperate with the inner work of your life you might feel as if you're never going to become a holy vessel for God. But, my dear friend, it's possible you already are and just don't see the beauty of who you have become in Christ.

For me, it's been more of a process cultivating a relationship with God. I've been through a lot with and without God in my life and everything in between. When I lived without Him I was lonely, lost and always searching for some<u>thing</u>. That something was really some<u>one</u>. Jesus Christ though I didn't know it then. Living in Him – abiding in Him- has made me peaceful, quiet, and confident. I've experienced both sides in life: light and darkness. Working out salvation and God's plan for our lives isn't always easy and there may be times when we can become disheartened and frustrated.

Maybe you (like me) have had times of being saved yet feeling lonely, lost and searching for something. All of us go through those dry, arid places of faith so we will not accept the status quo and dig deeper to find the treasure God has for us. Our treasure is Christ- he is the reward- and until this becomes our conclusion we will continue to search without finding what we've come for.

I think a dangerous place to be is constantly searching yet never finding because we are open to grabbing at scraps the enemy throws out there. The scraps are untruths made to look true, diversions, false doctrines and the like. They are easy pathways which seem right but provide no opportunity to build character in Christ. We grab at these because they look and sound good yet with possession of them we realize they have no power to heal or restore anything. These untruths are full of empty promises which like winding bunny trails took us way off track. Some were situations where our faith was pulverized as if we'd been in a meat grinder and in the worst sense have wasted our precious, finite time.

In the months leading up to our trip to China, my Bible reading was concentrated in the book of John. I was particularly focused on John 14:21(underline mine) and the word "manifest".

- ❖ "He that <u>hath</u> my commandments, and <u>keepeth</u> them, he it is that loveth me: and he that loveth me shall be loved of my Father, and I will love him, and will manifest myself to him."

What does it mean to have Christ manifest himself to me? A quick look in my concordance at the word manifest, reveals Jesus intends to declare and show himself openly and plainly to those who <u>have</u> and <u>keep</u> his commandments.[li] This is no ordinary promise. It is not empty but full of mutual love and holds the promise to see the Savior of the world clearly.

Most of the commentary I read about this verse replaces or uses the word obey for keeps and would read something like, "The person who has My commands and <u>obeys</u> them is the one who really loves Me…" But what if we're not seeing Christ manifest Himself in our lives? Could we conclude we're not being obedient to Christ? Would it mean our love for Him isn't real? Do we have to be perfectly obedient to every command in the Bible in order to love Christ and in turn be loved of the Father? What if we have good intentions trying methodically to obey every command of God without fail and still don't see Christ revealed in a personal way?

I think many of us do try to obey all the commands we read. The Word is our mirror and inspires and convicts us in many areas. Still, it can be overwhelming adding another area of transformation to our ever growing list of spiritual things we'd like to work on. I have moments when I think I can't possibly do everything I read in the Bible and become frustrated. But my frustration is not from God. He leads me to recognize my own sin and self but gives me hope to put my faith in Him to help in the restoration process. He never gives me more to work on than I can bear.

It's our satanic enemies who want us to feel overwhelmed with reformation to the point of quitting rather than advancing by faith. It's our own inner self who leads us to try and "do more" to change our outer, lower nature. We can try and change through religious memorization of Scripture or by forcing our will to be obedient. Generally we do this without taking into account it's impossible to follow every letter of the law in the flesh without the Spirit of God directing our path.

No matter how hard I try or want to change my flesh I find I cannot. I can certainly keep up my resolve for a while but eventually will make a mistake and wind up doing the very thing I don't want to do. Oh miserable me for trying to live my own way!

Don't get me wrong. I'm not saying memorization, recitation or even declaration of Scripture is wrong or even obedience to Christ and His Word is something we should quit trying to do. Of course we should do all those things <u>in their time</u> but we cannot use them to create our own sacrifice out of a religious spirit. We were crucified <u>with</u> Christ- not apart from him. Sanctification is a dead work if we are trying to be our own holy spirit.

How do we grow into a deeper faith moving past the Pharisaical trap so clearly defined and smashed by Jesus? The Pharisaical trap was about doing external things which made them look good like blowing a trumpet when they gave to the poor or wearing their clothes in a certain way. They thought these external observances of religious activity made them look good to men and God. Have we fallen into the same trap and thought religious activity whether prayer, service in ministry, church attendance, and observance of Christian holidays has made us acceptable and loved of the Father?

I think there is more to the verse from John and our life of faith than simply obedience. To me, obedience is more like a qualifier for advancement. We are trained by and through obedience after which it's time to delve deeper and go beyond the elementary doctrines of faith. To go deeper into anything of God requires a move toward the strongest force in the universe which is love.

I believe love underscores everything in faith. Love leads us to obey in a way our own self-will can never understand. As we grow up in faith it's important we walk by the Spirit and follow His lead on when and how to become the person He desires us to be. Anyone can set out to obey God's Word trying to follow a precept to the letter but I will repeat it again

<u>- in the flesh this is impossible to do and we will fail every time</u>. Are you tired of feeling miserable because you want to change and despite trying your best you wind up repeating the same old thing? Or have you thought maybe the Word just wasn't going to work for you and there must be some other way?

I'm right there with you. Lately I've begun my day thinking "today is the day everything will be different". I have been trying to make a change in my life and the more I try the more frustrated I get. My frustration has led me to everything from apathy, to anger, to feeling like I need a new life. At the very same time how right and wretched can my soul be.

It <u>is</u> a new life I need but not a physical one. There is nothing wrong with my life other than I've been trying to change it out of my flesh. I was trying to recite Scripture thinking it would change my outward self and what I was doing. What I needed to do was get back on the path of making change effectual as God has already shown me by working on who I'm being. My inner man must change first.

As much as I pray this book will help you- I know it is helping me. I desperately need the very words I've been writing. God allowed me to be frustrated to the point I threw up my arms and said "I give up- I don't know what to do anymore!" At the moment I gave up trying to change my self (even though it felt like the right thing to do) I saw the truth. I was trying to follow the letter of the law and not the law of the Spirit.

What we have begun in the Spirit cannot be finished in the flesh. We have no capability to save ourselves any more than we can sanctify ourselves. Change from the outside in is not really change at all. At best it is a mask we use to keep our real self hidden and comfortable from the pain of facing who we really are.

If you read the seventh chapter of Romans, Paul tells us it's impossible to change ourselves, "nothing good dwells within me, that is, in my flesh. I can will what is right, but I cannot perform it. (I have the intention and urge to do what is right, but no power to carry it out)."[lii]

To become who we were created to be requires a shift in focus from our fleshly man to our spirit man. The power to change doesn't come from our will or our want to do something but power comes from Love (Gods love for us and our love for Him) which leads to obedience to the Holy Spirit. By doing things that train us to obey like reading and memorization of the Word through the process of time we will become people who inwardly <u>have</u> the precepts of Christ and become <u>keepers</u> of them waiting in patience for the time Love leads us to do something proving our outer man is following the thoughts of our inner man.

When this happens we have true peace between our inner world and our external circumstances because we are following God's plan to deal with what He wants us to at any given time. We cannot get distracted and try to change areas of our life which don't bear the desire of God to be changed at the moment. In other words stay focused on your personal God designed path and you will be victorious one step at a time.

Let's look again at John 14:21 AMP, "He that hath my commandments, and <u>keepeth</u> them, he it is that loveth me…" Who loves Jesus? The person that <u>has</u> His commandments or precepts and <u>keepeth</u> them.[liii] How do we keep His precepts in the Spirit without trying to do worthless works of the flesh?

Like the Apostle Paul, we acknowledge there is nothing good in our flesh and when we feel frustrated and ready to give up –stop and identify frustration! Name it and then look at what we've been trying to do under the guise of religion in our own fleshly way. Remember feeling our own worthlessness and helplessness should lead us to God not away from Him.

Do you see how kind God is? He has not given us a hard, frustrating work to do or demanded us to develop a plan for internal change. He's just asked us to have and keep His Word, be obedient and let His Holy Spirit do the rest.[liv]

The word keep from our verse signifies we have set ourselves on a "watch". Watching is guarding the Word we see and hear while keeping our eye upon it so we don't lose it. We are to serve the Word out of love, preserving and holding it fast.

Then we can become obedient keepers as we perceive how the Holy Spirit would prompt us to act. When we act from the leading of the Holy Spirit we'll always be in the will of God and have the power to carry out our desires producing lasting fruit because now it is a matter of <u>love</u> and not <u>law</u>. Its love for God that leads us to obey. When we love God so much we'll obey Him more than our own flesh- watch out world!

Using our life to perceive Christ while striving to make our flesh obey gives us an assurance of knowing He loves us and so does the Father. Then Jesus will manifest Himself. Manifest has a twofold meaning. Jesus will either make himself clear to our eyes or mind and/or He can demonstrate the reality of the existence of what you're praying to see. Any way you look at it we'll have more light and be able to live with a greater spiritual sight than what we had before.

New spiritual sight will come in different forms like being a <u>knower</u> rather than a <u>believer</u>. You might suddenly become aware of Christ in your mind as never before and you may see into the spiritual realm. You'll change your mind on things if it conflicts with this newly revealed manifestation of Christ and you'll become so steadfast in your beliefs you can turn from useless works.

I will caution you -you could get off track if you desire Christ to manifest Himself through a vision for selfish reasons. Our motives should be pure and we need to understand the fine line between true prophecy and the occult. We shouldn't ask for visions because we don't want to open ourselves up to contrived satanic visions. As a masquerader of light, Satan can show someone a view into the spiritual realm. But it will be his altered view into a counterfeit kingdom not the real deal.

We are not in the business of selfishness or frivolity but are powerful God seekers enlisted in our time to pave the way for the Second Coming of His Son. Every way He shows Himself to you means something for your life or the life of someone else now or in the future.

We need clear sight, visions and prophecy for several reasons. Revelation 19:10 AMP says, "...Worship God! For the substance (essence) of the truth revealed by Jesus is the spirit of all prophecy [the vital breath, the inspiration of all inspired preaching and interpretation of the divine will and purpose, including both mine and yours]."

This is a powerful statement. First and foremost we should worship God not any other created object or being. Next we see even angels need God's will and purpose to be revealed by the truth that comes from Jesus. Prophecy is truth revealed by Jesus and is used to teach, preach and to <u>interpret God's will and purpose for ourselves and others</u>. If we want to live with purpose and help others interpret their purpose then it must be revealed through Christ.

Once during a church service I was touched by a prophetic word spoken by my Pastor. He spoke over the entire congregation, "your latter (days) will be greater than your past." At the end of the service he called up anyone who felt they couldn't connect with their purpose because they lacked confidence. I went forward as did hundreds of others. He looked over the group and commented we would be the last people others would expect to lack confidence because we were leaders.

He prayed for all of us and this prophecy was the inspired, revealed Word of God which gave me understanding into why I couldn't move into my purpose. I was being hindered by a false internal feeling about myself and needed encouragement that one day with Gods help I would overcome my lack of confidence and become the woman God created me to be. I needed something Divine to touch my inner spirit and God did through another who was obedient in love to speak the truth.

At this very moment God is willing to do the same for you. He will come along side you right now to strengthen your spirit so you can overcome all hindrances. He wants you to understand the workings of flesh and spirit so you can put away old, frustrating habits to start fresh and walk by His Spirit and begin to truly grasp your calling.

He desires to manifest Himself to you right now by giving you a new image of who Christ is in you. This new image will place a demand on you to choose to believe something you've not before. You cannot focus on the way things are now and expect to get to a new place of maturity. Instead turn a blind eye to what your natural eyes see and just start walking toward the direction of what Christ has revealed to you.

The prophecy I just wrote of changed my life and still speaks to me today. Over the years I have received similar encouragement through inspired books, church services, Scripture passages and personal meditation. I have them written down but they are scattered in many notebooks. Recently I read a newsletter from a pastor who suggested we put all of those important words of encouragement, visions and dreams into one notebook and call it our "blueprint".[lv]

He suggests we should look over our blueprint often, praying over it and speaking it aloud because these are the inspired and revealed ideas God has for us and by looking at them we will be encouraged to keep going in times of struggle. He wrote further stating this is one way we can be good ground and hold on to the Word we hear without having it stolen by our enemy. He quoted Luke 8:15: "But that on the good ground are they, which in an honest and good heart, <u>having heard the word, keep it, and bring forth fruit with patience</u>."

When I saw that verse I about jumped out of my skin for joy. It's the pattern I've been writing about and parallels our verse from John. We hear the Word - keep it and whether it be clear skies or stormy weather we hold fast to <u>that</u> word. And the great end of this verse says through <u>patience</u> we will bring forth fruit.

I'm thrilled to have this promise because not all fruit is evident immediately. Some fruit takes more time and requires more from us in order to ripen. Often in my time alone with God I wonder about what fruit there might be from my life. Like me, I hope you take great consolation if you are living and doing right, hearing and holding on to God's revealed wisdom for your life, in due time if you pursue His grand plan through patience you will produce a crop of fruit. Don't give up not for a minute in this life doing what you know to do by the Holy Spirt because real fruit is eternal and it will bear a crop even after you are gone.

Lastly, I think we need to see into Heaven to help us live our everyday lives. Every time I've had a vision or dream from God in my personal prayer time I would put it in the category of being amazing. We've all been in church services or attended conferences where faith rose so high we felt anything was possible. And then we leave the place of faith and come back in contact with our life and could hear a sound like nails screeching down a black board. We would all love to stay in our faith cocoon but then how would we walk out what we'd just been privileged to hear and see?

Even Jesus had to leave the Mount of Transfiguration and come down off of it to deal with people. Jesus had just been glorified as God and spoke to Moses and Elijah only to leave and enter into an argument already in progression. We need the high spiritual experiences to outlive the low and mundane times. We can do repetitive work in a new way after a high spiritual experience because we are open to looking at things differently. Also, our work keeps us humble and connected with the rest of humanity.

Because I saw Heaven in a vision, I'm confident in my indestructible relationship with the Almighty. I don't just know God but am known <u>by</u> God. I am known and you are known. As you are known so also is your individualized purpose. It's being kept for the exact right time in history.

I lived my entire life to stand at the bar in front of the Throne of Grace. From birth every single experience no matter what it was moved me closer to that moment. I now see my life as before and after the vision. Everything before is now gone in the sense it served its purpose. Everything after is changed because I accepted Jesus as He was revealed to me. He is truly All-Sufficient in His power working mightily in and toward all of us who believe and call upon His Name. I hope through my experience in China you see and know nothing in your life whether it be past or present will be wasted. No sacrifice you offer through Christ to God goes unnoticed.

God absolutely loves you. You are the apple of His eye. He adores you for thinking about Him when you could be thinking about any number of things. He loves when you read and think on His word every chance you get. He loves when you get upset over missing your time with Him. He's attentive to you because you are attentive to Him. He's already showered you with every heavenly blessing which exists and waits patiently with great expectance for you to unwrap the promises He has carefully hidden for you.

Tell your heart to be still and treasure what He would say to you right now. Write it down and keep watch over what He speaks to you. You are ever before Him as your life stands as a lighted pillar of His grace in a dark world. Amen!

LIGHT FROM A DARK NIGHT

15 Accepting Christ as Revealed

Being weak is not a position we would normally choose for ourselves. No one wants to be without wealth, influence or resources especially in a situation where you need something of value to offer or barter with to get results. We are used to making things happen for ourselves. But as we take in lessons from the Bible we learn God delights to make the weak things of the world strong to amaze the wise. Our weakness actually turns into something God can use to show the world His love and power.

An orphan like Bella was alone, without wealth, status, or power. Yet God loved her so much even before she was born and had a plan in place for her life. Let's dwell on this line of thinking for a minute. Since God is no respecter of persons we can apply this to our own lives. He loved us before we were born and had a life plan in place for us too. For we've all been in the position of an orphan; weak, powerless, poor, vulnerable and alone stumbling around in a dark world until Christ became our great Savior and Advocate. He has done what we could not do for ourselves therefore our dependence upon Him is to be extreme and is vitally necessary for life. Living as salt and light in a dark world we are still vulnerable to the dominion of darkness that rules the earth. However we are not alone, poor or powerless. If we allow ourselves to become weak to put on Christ's strength then the world will see the manifestation of God's love and power resting upon us.

This awesome power won't rest on us unless we become humble understanding the frailty of being human. The work of the Holy Spirit is to reveal to us <u>ourselves</u> and <u>Christ</u>. We must know who we really are to see our own lack and to feel what of Christ's we are still missing. If we always feel full of our own self and ability then the Holy Spirit cannot reveal Christ to us because the need of Him is not present.

How much do we miss of Christ because we don't know our deep need for Him? But our need to know Christ becomes clearer through experiences which test us. Sometimes we need to go through something or be put into a circumstance to bring out our real need for God which might be overlooked in the ordinary setting of everyday life. When we allow ourselves to feel things like emptiness, loneliness, or abandonment in the spirit of knowing our need of Christ then the Holy Spirit can reveal Christ. You must feel your need or emptiness in order to recognize the feeling of being filled and full.

Think of it in natural terms. How do you know when you've really fallen in love with someone? How would you recognize the difference between infatuation and love? Knowledge comes from experiencing them both. Maybe you've experienced crazy passion for someone confusing it to be love until true love comes along. After experiencing them both you know the difference between the two feelings.

It's the same with salvation. Before salvation you didn't give much thought of God and your need for Him. But through an experience you came to know the painful emptiness of your own self in order to recognize the wondrous feeling of being filled with a peace which surpasses all you'd known before.

In both these instances we must feel the one in order to recognize the other. I think Charles Finney wrote it best, "The glory and fullness of Christ are not discovered to the soul, until it discovers its need for him."[lvi] He goes on to write: "what we know of Christ corresponds directly to our necessity of Him and if we accept who He is revealed by faith then a great work is done."

For the work to be complete we must accept who Christ is as revealed to us by the Holy Spirit. In my case, He was revealed as my All Sufficiency. For the work to become complete I had to keep myself from trying to do anything in my own strength and power. I had to trust God with my whole heart and being. Proverbs 3: 5-6 says,

"Lean on, trust in, and be confident in the Lord with all your heart and mind and do not rely on your own insight or understanding. In all your ways know, recognize, and acknowledge Him, and He will direct and make straight and plain your paths."

I trusted God with my heart and mind which opened up the way for Him to direct my path. At the time it seemed difficult to keep myself from doing something to get Bella's medical clearance but looking back it was easy. All I had to do was keep watch, wait on His purposes and act when it was time. He did all the work. I have no idea how hard things might have become if I'd intervened in some way.

Place your trust in His Sufficiency for your life. Let Him do the work. As you wait on Him and watch for Him your destiny will unfold.

LIGHT FROM A DARK NIGHT

16 The Power of Words and Thoughts

While praying in the Chinese hospital, I used my mind to recount the wonders and deliverances God made available to the saints in the Bible. I concluded I had to know God in this way for myself. I wanted God to rescue and manifest Himself to me as my husband and hero. I would not be content until I had what I was asking for.

My thoughts were concentrated on God. This is important because I could have been thinking about anything else. I could have focused my thoughts on how unfair the system was or on ways we could get ourselves out of the jam we were in. I believe our thoughts have more to do with our power and authority as a believer as well as answered prayer than we currently realize.

Remember just before I saw the vision into heaven; "I retreated into my own thoughts about Jesus and the attacks from the demon(s) stopped?" I didn't really know why they stopped just I ceased to care about them when compared to thinking about Jesus. I didn't have to say a word. I didn't have to scream out a loud rebuke. Could my thoughts toward Christ have drowned out and shut up the enemy?

If so, this would be a giant revelation. In all my times of verbal declarations for the things of God and rebuke of the enemy I took notice my volume would escalate when talking to the enemy. Do Satan and those in the spiritual world respond to our raised voices and verbal commands?

Adding to my growing list of questions I wondered how it was possible for us to hear individually from angels, demons and even God himself when no one else around us hears. How was it I heard screaming demon voices in our hotel room which never woke up Rob or Bella? How could I hear their shrieks in the hospital yet no one else heard them? Recently while reading a book by Praying Medic I received insight. In his book "Seeing in the Spirit made Simple" he explains, "Spirit beings don't speak in audible voices through vocal chords that use sound waves. They speak spirit to spirit and can target and manifest in appearance to specific individuals yet remain concealed to others." (My paraphrase of his words in quotations)

He goes on to explain our thoughts emit light or darkness depending on our inner spiritual life and they are visible to the spiritual world. Aha! Confirmation of what I wrote previously. Our thoughts do go somewhere- they rise from our being! Our thoughts are being heard- not necessarily the specific words we are thinking in our own language but our thoughts surround us and rise as light or darkness.

Our thoughts confirm the real person of our inner man.

Communication with the spiritual realm is happening on a level we are mostly unaware of. Our spirit is interfacing in another dimension with other spirit beings at all times and our inner being whether it is light or dark is clearly seen. Our thoughts are our real inner person and they don't lie like our words can.

With words we can conceal and cover up our true feelings from another which is a kind way of saying we lie to others. We can tell someone they "didn't hurt our feelings" when our thoughts tell another story. Sometimes our feelings <u>have been hurt</u> but we <u>don't want to say so</u>. There have been times when I've told my husband, "I'll do the supper dishes, I don't mind". Then, while doing what I said "I didn't mind", my thoughts recount all the ways I'm being taking advantage of as a mother and wife. Truthfully, I did mind but I concealed my feelings.

This isn't always wrong as I'm not advocating we speak out destructive thoughts. But what I want you to see clearly is our inner being doesn't conceal itself -from our self. If we really do mind something like doing the dishes, our inner self knows this to be true as opposed to what we just said. Our inner being is our true self and we can conceal it at will for various reasons to other people like us living in the physical world.

However, we cannot hide anything before God – all is laid bare. He knows us by our true inner self no matter what we have done or are currently doing. Even what we are doing in ministry. We can heal the sick, prophesy in His name and a host of other things and it is still possible for Him to say, "Depart from me, I never knew you". The real you he may never know is your thought life. Do your thoughts bring you closer to Him or do you say one thing while your heart is far from Him? Can God see your inner being as light?

As a physical being on earth our words of faith carry power because this is our method of communication. We make declarations, speak to the mountain, prophesy encouragement to others, bind and loose. There is power in our tongue to bless or curse. In the spiritual world our words and thoughts carry power. Who responds to them and in what way depends on if our inner light is truly light and not dark. Satan can't read your mind- just the light or dark coming from your thoughts. Again, our specific thoughts aren't being "read" by angels and demons just <u>seen</u> as being light or dark. Our thoughts tell the tale of what we really think and they may reveal fear, doubt, or the strength of our faith in particular areas to angels and demons alike.

Are you beginning to see the disconnect we have with trying to rebuke demons and command them to leave and so forth with words when we don't have the inner light (belief) to do so? A demon will not leave you alone because you tell him to "Go!" unless he sees your thoughts (light that radiates in the spiritual realm from your person) match your words. You cannot be double minded with spiritual beings saying one thing and thinking another and carry any kind of power. Your words may be making a sound but your thoughts are seen and tell the true tale.

Now track with me here. You will get this all wrong if you think I'm proposing we don't speak out loud to rebuke demons or to pray. Additionally I'm not suggesting we "think good thoughts" as in the New Age Movement or Self Help methods advocate. A person can think good thoughts all they want but again -our inner light or darkness tells whether we are God's child or not. Our spirit is either lit up or it is completely dark.

God wants you to understand how to operate creatively and prosper as a spirit being living in a physical world. This is essential knowledge for you to become whole and fulfill your divine calling. Now is the time for your voice to be heard- silence is for the grave.

Remember the seven sons of Sceva from Acts 19? They were men trying to cast out demons using the name of "the God Paul knew" but had no inward relationship with Jesus Christ. The demons spoke and said they knew Jesus and Paul but not these men. The demons controlled the helpless man to overpower the sons of Sceva.

These sons of Sceva had no inner light. Their spirit was not awakened. What they did have was the desire to be powerful like Paul. But you cannot display power in the natural realm if you don't possess it in the spiritual. Your light is your power. Your light is a lighted spirit man who is seen by those in the spiritual realm – angels and demons alike. Only those who are born again have a spirit who is fully awake and seated with Christ. We are known in heaven because we are seen there. You are known in heaven because you've been there by your spirit.

Looking back at my experience with the demons in the hotel and the hospital I felt a frightening fear in both places. A fear that made me shake and feel like my life was in imminent danger. What I know now is my fear was sensed by the demon in the spirit realm through my thoughts and gave him the go ahead to keep pressing me. Fear created a dark light attracting more fear.

I thought if I ignored the situation and looked like I wasn't afraid the demon(s) would go away and fear would leave me. But fear did not leave because I really was afraid -internally. In the physical world we are able to feel fear while trying to disguise it externally. That may work on earth because others cannot know what is truly going on inside. In the spiritual realm, our fear is seen no matter what we do or say to prove otherwise. Only after I meditated on God being present in my life through everything did fear leave. In the hospital it was the same thing, my thoughts of Christ shut off the fear in me and the enemy saw dark turn to light in the spirit realm and left. Perfect love really does cast out all fear!

We know to resist Satan and he will flee from us but how do we resist? I always thought this verse was telling us to use our voice for a strong rebuke but does this always work? Can we command the enemy sharply (often loudly) and he obeys? We've read of Jesus who spoke the Word of God in response to Satan while being tempted in the wilderness and Satan left him. Jesus rebuked Satan's influence over Peter and rebuked the storm while on a boat. To imitate Christ we can and should use our voice to rebuke Satan but why don't we have the same success rate?

I believe it's because our heart and thoughts don't match our words. Jesus' words matched his heart and thoughts. He had the radiating light coming from his being. When he told someone they were healed, they were healed. He didn't say they were healed and doubt the power of God to do the work.

His entire being spirit, soul and body was in unison and could move in power because of it. We can have His same power in the earth today in our sphere of influence when we become a whole being. Our words will be potent and hit bullseye when the light radiating from our thoughts proves our inner conviction in whatever area we set our heart on.

Our heart must produce thoughts in agreement with our words so our personal light seen in the spiritual realm is light and not dark.

We can no longer say one thing but think another and expect victory over the enemy. Our wrestling with temptation and sin is won in our soul. Our mind and self-will have to be in agreement with our words against addiction, temptation, and sin or we will not overpower them. For instance, to please someone you say you'll quit smoking but your internal self-will isn't in agreement with those words. Guess what? You will remain addicted to cigarettes until you have the complete conviction of your will to do it. Understanding your being as tri-part and delving into how you are made by God would be time well spent. In so doing you will find yourself less confused and possessing greater authority in Christ.

Now let's take a look at angels. When I found myself in the courtroom of God I felt like I knew specifically what to ask for, "…as many angels as God would release into my command to do what we could not, to move on the one doctor who would be open to the Holy Spirit". When the vision ended I was at peace knowing angels were working on our behalf. This puzzled me for quite some time. Weren't angels already working for me? Aren't they helping me at all times? I knew I hadn't asked amiss in Heaven but why was I sure angels were specifically working for me after the vision but not before?

Angels minister to heirs of salvation. They can be loosed on our behalf and respond to His Word. They will not do anything that doesn't line up with God's Word. From the book of Daniel we know they can be resisted by Satan and his forces too. This battle was being fought in the spiritual realm based on prayers from one man. God released a mighty angel to come help push against the evil forces so an answer might get through to Daniel.

> ❖ "So he said to me, "O Daniel, you highly regarded *and* greatly beloved man, understand the words that I am about to say to you and stand upright, for I have now been sent to you." And while he was saying this word to me, I stood up trembling.[12] Then he said to me, "Do not be afraid, Daniel, for from the first day that you set your heart on understanding this and on humbling yourself before your God, your words were heard, and I have come in response to your words. [13] But the [e]prince of the kingdom of Persia was standing in opposition to me for twenty-one days. Then, behold, Michael, one of the chief [of the celestial] princes, came to help me, for I had been left there with the kings of Persia. [14] Now I have come to make you understand what will happen to your people in the latter days, for the vision is in regard to the days yet to come."[lvii]

I'd like you to look at some words from these verses. Notice the angel said "now" he was sent; "now" I have come. And why was he sent? Because Daniel set his heart and mind on God <u>and</u> he spoke words of faith. An angel was sent to him because of his words and Daniel had the internal power of having a set mind in agreement with those words coupled with persistence. Daniel was steadfast in His petition to God for an answer to understand a troubling vision.

It is the same with us today, answers to our prayers are being sent but can be fought and resisted successfully by forces of darkness in the spiritual realm. If we are persistent and do not give up seeking God for wisdom and an answer- we will get it. Angels will continue to fight for you as long as they see light shining from your spirit. When you give up seeking God for whatever reason your light for that particular thing shuts off. If you give up and no longer are using your faith to fight then why should they continue on for you?

In my case, I believe angels were helping me but being fought and detained by spiritual forces of darkness. I myself was wrestling with beings in the spirit realm but needed special help from a particular class of angel. This special class of angel are the weapons which are mighty for the pulling down of strongholds. In the spirit we wrestle against enemies who are not flesh and blood but it is the angelic beings who fight the battles with mighty weapons.

Angels have a tongue or language of their own but can understand you through your spirit to theirs. God restored communication by the Spirit as we read about in the book of Acts. Spiritual men understand spiritual language. Our soul is capable of interpreting spiritual and non-spiritual language into something we can understand.

And what if we could speak the language of angels? Would that help us in our walk of faith? Not if we don't have love. 1 Corinthians 13 says:

> ❖ If I speak with the tongues of men and of angels, but have not [a]love [for others growing out of God's love for me], then I have become only a noisy gong or a clanging cymbal [just an annoying distraction]. 2 And if I have *the gift of* prophecy [and speak a new message from God to the people], and understand all mysteries, and [possess] all knowledge; and if I have all [sufficient] faith so that I can remove mountains, but do not have love [reaching out to others], I am nothing. 3 If I give all my possessions to feed *the poor*, and if I surrender my body [b]to be burned, but do not have love, it does me no good at all.

Without love what is heard from our mouths? Irritating noise! That's how we sound in the spiritual realm if we don't have love. Think how noisy we may be- praying with our words yet the only sound being heard is loud banging if the love of God for others is not really in our hearts. We think we're speaking light but if love is not in us our words of light are seen as darkness and heard as noise.

It's possible we are not as powerful as we want to be nor do we carry as much authority as we'd like because we don't have corresponding thoughts to match our words. Our individual light seen in the heavenly may not be as bright as it could be. Not only does this apply to us individually but corporately as the Church.

The Church in America is not as powerful as it could be because many of its members are not emitting any light. The light in some of us is dark (see Matt. 6:22-23) and Jesus said <u>if the light in you is dark then great is your darkness</u>.

We live in a time when strength seems to be in the numbers. Social media has connected the world and millions can see the same video or read the same tweet. Corporations are changing policy due to social activism – some of it good and some not so good- based on volume of responders to social sites. The Church can get caught up in numbers too thinking the more who are with us the stronger we are. But are large numbers making us more powerful?

Many say they are part of the Church. But if we really had power and authority our nation would not be a nation under such moral distress. Many have allowed themselves to sit under a lesser umbrella of authority whether it be Democrat, Republican, Independent or whatever as opposed to being under the rule of God and His authority. We have made our political party an idol if we say we believe in God outwardly yet inwardly follow our party even when they go against the morals of God.

What about the people who are truly crying out to God to save us from becoming a godless country? Wondering when will God act? When will He do something? These questions cause me to think a little bit. Have we – those of us in the Church - wearied or offended God in some way?

Maybe we have by not living up to our great calling to be kings and priests.

> ❖ So I, the prisoner for the Lord, appeal to you to live a life worthy of the calling to which you have been called [that is, to live a life that exhibits godly character, moral courage, personal integrity, and mature behavior — a life that expresses gratitude to God for your salvation], 2 with all humility [forsaking self-righteousness], and gentleness [maintaining self-control], with patience, bearing with one another [a]in [unselfish] love.[lviii]

Paul suggests we should live a life worthy of our calling and gives us four ways to do that: humility, gentleness, patience, and bearing with each other in love.

We might be saying the right thing and outwardly appearing to others as doing right but in our inner world where our true self resides is there darkness coming forth as light? A person in this state will have no power or authority to win battles in the spiritual realm and will live a life of defeat. They may even think, "Christianity doesn't work for me".

In the book of Malachi 3: 1-5 God diagnoses some of the reasons why the Israelite's prayers were not being answered. We could ask ourselves the same questions. Are we dealing faithfully with God bringing him the honour he deserves as our Father and Master? Are we being faithful in our dealings with others – bearing with them in love? Are we faithful to our marriage covenants? We need to make some things right quickly because it is hard for God to bring justice near to us when those we have offended are crying out to him for justice against us. God gives us Christ as the solution for He will purify and refine so our offerings will be received and pleasing again.[lix]

Christ is our refiner and places us in a process to cleanse us of impurities so we can be pleasing and walk worthy of His calling. Peter tells us we are a "special priesthood". It is our job now to offer spiritual sacrifices to God after we have been cleansed by Christ.

We have been calling out for God's justice and help yet as a collective Church refuse to do the inward work necessary to fulfill our calling of being a royal priesthood. If we won't be refined by being placed in the fire how can we offer ourselves up as pleasing to God in Christ?

If we would humble ourselves before God and offer acceptable sacrifices to him- especially those who are born afresh then He will come swiftly near to judge as we seek.

- ❖ "Then I will draw near to you for judgment; I will be a swift witness against the sorcerers, against the adulterers, against the false swearers, and against those who oppress the hireling in his wages, the widow and the fatherless, and who turn aside the temporary resident from his right and fear not Me, says the Lord of hosts."[lx]

If the light of the Church would truly be light we would carry power and authority in the Spiritual realm which would make the workers of darkness back up in fear.

Our prayers will be answered more readily when we have agreement between our words of faith and our heart. Speaking to the mountains is only half of the equation. If we want to see them move we can't doubt in our hearts at the same time.

Not long ago I saw a vision and it went like this:

- "I was walking in a dense, dark forest with very few rays of light coming through the trees. These few rays of light were revelations and a few rays of hope. I came upon the edge of this forest which was covered with very thick foliage. I parted the foliage to peer through and saw pure light.

    I backed up and thought about the edge of the forest being such a thick hedge. I realized I was being given a chance along with others to leave the dark forest and live in the light. I had to make a decision: move into the light or go back to the forest.

I parted the hedge once more and stepped through to pure light- pure revelation.

I looked back at the forest. I was no longer in it but above it. Looking down at the forest I saw it was covered with deep black clouds- utter blackness. Suddenly I saw the forest was made of people. I began to cry. I said, "Lord, I love this place (the light) but I cannot leave them there in darkness."

I turned around to face the forest and remembered another vision the Lord had given me so many years ago. This was that!

I stood in a sphere of pure light facing the darkness covering the forest. Suddenly I was connected to other people forming a line around the perimeter of this sphere of light. We were not there to block others from coming into the light but had become part of the pure light.

In fact the whole sphere was comprised with people of light but we were not seen as individuals just complete light."

The Lord told me this sphere- a sphere of light is Truth. It is a truth of His you buy and live. Once inside you become part of its light. Others who peer through the dense hedge as I did won't see any of the other people just the light. Each will have to make a decision to leave the forest on their own without the influence of seeing others who have also made the choice. Once in the light and joined with others the sphere will push outward and make the darkness in the forest a thin ring.

Coming to the hedge is like coming to the edge of a promise you see in God's word which you are making a decision to believe or not. Do you believe in healing? Then walk through the hedge and become part of the light. Do you believe all things are possible with God? Then walk through the hedge into the sphere of Truth joining with others to push back the darkness the enemy uses against people keeping them bound.

One mistake I made was thinking the people living in the dark forest were the unsaved. Not so, the people of the forest were the saved. It is God's own people who are living in relative darkness; confused yet satisfied with very little light. Many have no idea they could be living in greater clarity and wholeness and instead remain where they are rather than take a chance by looking more closely at God.

My part, along with those in the sphere of light, is to set my heart and mind on God who has taken us out of darkness and placed us into his light so we can show the world his goodness. We decree the dark cloud the enemy has placed over God's people be removed so God's people can see clearly into the spiritual realm. How else can we show the world His goodness? The only way to bring Heaven to Earth is to see Heaven. Any other good things we do are man's earthly ideas and will be useless dead works.

Please believe me- God does not want you to be in the dark all the time. He doesn't want you feeling like you can't see what He has called <u>you</u> to see. None of us will see <u>all things</u> clear and perfect but each of us has been called to see <u>something</u> clearly so we can share it with the body of Christ and the world. Individual spheres of light brought together collectively will reveal a much greater whole.

In Ephesians 2, we read about our true place in this life, now- not the sweet by and by - is to be seated in the <u>heavenly sphere</u>! We are meant to have influence over and in the affairs of this earth. We are meant to command armies of angels. In Christ we are supposed to be above the darkness to be a person who is on display to show the world now and in the age to come just how limitless and rich in mercy our God is.

We are readers of the Word and desire to see the "greater works" spoken of by Christ. The will to do them and the desire in us is from God. The power to do them is ready when we agree with and begin walking in our Purpose. He chooses those who will patiently wait to perform these greater works as he has determined.

But make no mistake – your desire to become one who is not just called but chosen will place you on a path to be refined in the fire as much as is necessary and determined by Christ. He is the Author and the Completer of our faith. We shouldn't be unaware of this process wondering what is wrong with our faith. Instead embrace the process of being conformed into the image of Christ!

And the more we think (meditate and behold) Christ the more light we'll possess and emit. Every time you use your mind to think about God with thoughts of praise, worship or reflection or use your will to deny what you want for his sake and glory– <u>He is pleased</u>! Every thought of light is a personal love letter to God. A Letter of Light!

I know you haven't come all this way with me for nothing so I want to give you more pertaining to the sphere of light. Philippians 2:14-15 (underline mine):

- ❖ "Do everything without murmuring or questioning [the providence of God], [15] so that you may prove yourselves to be blameless *and* guileless, innocent *and* uncontaminated, children of God without blemish in the midst of a [morally] crooked and [spiritually] perverted generation, <u>among whom you are seen as bright lights</u> [beacons shining out clearly] in the world [of darkness],…"

I've read this before but today it stands out as a defining Word to everyone who will take it and assimilate it into their life. I always thought Paul was talking about our grumbling as we go about our daily lives. I admit to my share of complaining and since I've been writing this book I am able to recognize it quicker and stop the flow in my head- because my heart has changed. I want my thoughts to be pure and seen as light upon me.

We are certainly heading in the right direction doing so but I'd like you to see an aspect of this verse I never considered until now. I believe we are to do everything God asks of us- without questioning his will and without complaining especially while doing ministry work.

What makes the above generation or nation (as it reads in the KJV) crooked and perverse? They are crooked in their paths- hard to deal with, unhappy, and marked by trouble. We live among perverse people which means they are morally corrupt, distort verses in the Bible and misinterpret spiritual matters.

It is not God who cannot or will not be known among them but it is they who will not know God.

Therefore, the crooked generation have set themselves against God. Everything wrong in their lives becomes God's fault including the fact he made them male or female when they want to be the opposite.

God will however have a people – a nation within a nation- on the earth who long for him, who love and worship him and celebrate his Divine hand in their lives. We are the "peculiar people"[lxi] who pursue godliness and must make it our aim to be happy and content with living and doing whatever God has given us to do.

God is our reward- in fact an exceeding great reward. This should satisfy us beyond any earthly wealth. God passionately looks for and is pleased with those who are satisfied with Him and in Him. To you He has given <u>all riches</u> of being able to see into His Word and the Spiritual Sphere. To you He has given the right to be a king- able to look into matters you have no breeding or education for.

Set your heart and mind to be satisfied with Christ. Not, "well if this is as good as it gets I guess I will be happy". But satisfied as in: pleased, happy, and triumphant. And no grumbling doing anything with your words or thoughts. If you need to work through some things – do so. Asking God or wondering about things is ok as long as you accept His answer knowing he is LOVE. Always remember there is time and space to grow in your faith.

If you feel like you don't measure up– don't worry and don't give up. Part of the dark cloud the enemy likes hanging over our heads is condemnation. There were times in my life when I'd be about my own business and suddenly feel like I had done something wrong. I knew I wasn't doing anything wrong but I felt like I had. Just the sensation of condemnation was enough to alter my day and keep me from feeling like I could do what God wanted me to do.

Condemnation is an enemy attack. It may be our spirit hears a satanic accusation from the "accuser of the brethren" and our soul tries to interpret this. Now if this happens to me; I'm quick to agree that I have sinned against God in some way. I ask for forgiveness of anything I did or thought whether I knew about it or not. And receive forgiveness. This way the enemy cannot continue to level an accusation against me and I can go on without being under a dark cloud.

God is calling his people to question their existence in the forest. Don't think this illustration is silly. God used the metaphor of his people being a forest in Ezekiel 20:45-48. He knows what he's talking about. God wants us to come out from under the authority of the dark cloud! I pray you are hearing because being in the sphere of light is more important than anything. Once you enter the sphere of light, you are "in the Father". You will have become a fulfilment of Jesus' words recorded for us in John 17:20-23 (THE MESSAGE):

"I'm praying not only for them
But also for those who will believe in me
Because of them and their witness about me.
The goal is for all of them to become one heart and mind —
Just as you, Father, are in me and I in you,
So they might be one heart and mind with us.
Then the world might believe that you, in fact, sent me.
The same glory you gave me, I gave them,

So they'll be as unified and together as we are —
I in them and you in me.
Then they'll be mature in this oneness,
And give the godless world evidence
That you've sent me and loved them
In the same way you've loved me."

The Father desires everyone to be "in Him". He desires to inhabit the praises of his people. The dark cloud covering the saints is nothing more than Satan inhabiting the dark thoughts coming from God's people. Our dark thoughts combined collectively are creating an atmosphere of heaviness and darkness above us which is why some have "little hope and a few revelations".

Being in the light is liberating. There is complete freedom. Freedom not to sin and be covered by grace but to be covered by grace and sin not. The reward for being in Him is you SHINE as LIGHTS in a dark world. Actually you shine as a LUMINARY- you are as bright as the sun or moon and are "a person who inspires or influences others, especially one prominent in a particular sphere."[lxii]

The light beams from your life will begin to attract and call others. You may not see it in the physical realm but it is existent at all times in the spiritual. Shine brilliantly and let your thoughts rise as light in ever increasing measure.

LIGHT FROM A DARK NIGHT

17 Become a Vessel to Rule

Wow- after writing last chapter I felt like I could soar forever! However, upon deciding to direct my thoughts to become light I hit some very intense spiritual push back. We had flare ups of anger and arguing as a family like we haven't experienced for a while. I felt like "all hell was breaking loose". And, it was breaking loose - right off my life and it will break off yours too if you stand firm.

I want you to be aware of enemy schemes so you will not quit pursuing God and taking stands of faith in increasing measure. The enemy doesn't like us to move deeper into God's light because we become stronger and understand how to destroy more of his works. Don't ever think God doesn't want you to move into a new sphere and operate in it by His Divine Design. This is for you! Especially operating in the sphere of being "in Him". We are in Christ as Christ was in the Father. From this vantage point you are seated with Christ in Heavenly places far above demonic rule and even above some levels of angels.

Because of this understanding we should expect to wrestle in the heavenly for our new way of life- which is to conquer not mankind but spiritual wickedness and all manner of evil in the name of Christ. Advancing in faith is worth it. The gates of hell cannot prevail against an <u>advancing</u> Church. Even though there was intense back lash at first, I still pursued God to think thoughts of light in worship to Him and have them manifest for my good and the good of others. I feel stronger in my spirit and enjoy using my thoughts for good purpose.

It wasn't always that way. For years I was like everyone else who lives under the power of the god of this world. I was disobedient to God and followed the desires and thoughts of my sinful nature. Paul said living this way made me (and you) by nature "objects of wrath".[lxiii] Now, I can follow my thoughts coming from an obedient heart and feel free to act on them because they are pleasing to God.

You might wonder how thoughts create the dark cloud of the enemy I wrote about last chapter. We know our thoughts rise. They ascend upward: some to the very throne of God and others never even reach Him. There are Seraphim and Cherubim two different types of angels at the Throne of God one with fire and one with praise. God is so holy and pure nothing sinful or un-holy may come near him without being destroyed. Un-holy thoughts of mankind aren't penetrating the being of God. He doesn't hold these thoughts in him like we would hold thoughts of bitterness, or resentment in our souls.

So thoughts like these and more from God's own believers don't go above the dark cloud I saw but stop and reside there. From these thoughts the enemy gains power and can "rain down" and return to the earth those same thoughts along with the consequences of them. So God's own people play a very important role in whether God's songs of virtue penetrate to mankind or whether the hatred being spewed by the demonic rulers are heard.

Until now I thought the demonic screams I heard on the night of my dark night of the soul were unusual. But now I believe they are being shouted down to us at all times from this dark cloud. We are just unable to hear them. That night I heard audibly what previously has been unheard or dismissed as imagination.

These screams are the design of Satan and are awful, frightening, hateful and terrifying accusations but that night I did bear some responsibility. My questions and thoughts had not been totally pure. I was in fear that night. I was questioning my faith and God's plan. I lingered over the accusations of the enemy. And with my lingering the enemies tirade became fiercer. In other words, my thoughts of this nature were not reaching the Throne of God. They were reaching the dark cloud and bouncing back to me with magnified intensity.

You might be thinking, "My thoughts aren't that bad" or "I'm not a murderer or anything". Well, Jesus taught you might be one if you think and or say something against another. Let's look at something Jesus said in the light of the vision of the dark cloud.

"You're familiar with the command to the ancients, 'Do not murder.' I'm telling you that anyone who is so much as angry with a brother or sister is guilty of murder. Carelessly call a brother 'idiot!' and you just might find yourself hauled into court. Thoughtlessly yell 'stupid!' at a sister and you are on the brink of hellfire. The simple moral fact is that words kill."
Matthew 5:21-22 THE MESSAGE

Words can kill. Where do our words come from? Our thoughts. Where do our thoughts come from? The meditation of our hearts. We absolutely must come to an understanding of our thoughts in connection to what is happening not only to us but those around us on earth. It would not hurt to ask forgiveness for our thoughts and words which have been dark. Dark thoughts are those which aren't of Heaven, aren't pure, excellent, of good report and so forth as described by the Apostle Paul in Philippians 4:8.

When we choose to meditate on something bad which happened to us- our thoughts follow this meditation. Eventually we will speak it out but whether we speak it verbally or not the thoughts we think have risen and join the dark cloud from which Satan the power of the air can operate.

The dark cloud can become so dark the penetration of light and revelation becomes all but nonexistent to those under it. Lack of light in a deep, dense forest produces confusion, death and decay. Light is revelation. Therefore lack of light (or revelation) to believers produces confusion, death of purpose which leads to decay producing dead works of the flesh.

Choosing to meditate on those good things which are excellent and of Heaven allows light and revelation to shine down upon us. In an earlier chapter I wrote of the summer vacation we spent in Hilton Head. I used my free time or shall I say free thought time while on the beach to think about God. This pleased God because I could have been thinking about absolutely anything else except how much I loved Him.

Unclean thoughts keep us from being "in Him". Yet everything we want or need is "in Him" and so it is a clever design of the enemy to keep us from receiving all which is meant for us by not understanding the power of our thoughts and words.

Once I was manning a table in which we were selling tickets for a ministry event. I was setting up with another lady before service while the worship team did sound checks. When the sound check ended a member of the worship team came to the table. I thought he was there to purchase a ticket. Instead he verbally accused the other lady of something and the whole scene was ugly. At the start of service he went right back up on stage; smiled and sang through the whole service.

Unless he repented - his worship could not even get to the Throne of God. His words stemming from prior meditation of the heart and thoughts rose to the dark cloud and not above it. We have to stop being double minded. <u>The double minded do not receive anything.</u>

This is something I hope we all change after reading this book. We should watch the unhealthy meditations of our hearts knowing they could eventually lead to words and prayers never going beyond the dark cloud. Let's begin to stop unhealthy thoughts in their tracks. Stop them, repent, loose them from our souls. If it's a strong unhealthy belief system continue to loose it as many times as necessary. If you are just beginning to change unhealthy thoughts, you might have a saying handy or a song to recite or sing to quickly change your thinking. As you do, push back the darkness with truth and more of God's light and revelation will penetrate even the darkest places of confusion.

Each day I see more and more I want to share. Writing to you has become part of my life which I love- it is hard for me to stop! But I sense it's time for me to start wrapping up and let you move into a new place of purpose.

If you get a chance to read "There Were Two Trees in the Garden" by Rick Joyner I would do so. About half way through the book I read this about Satan, "Knowing that Jesus was to be the heir of the world, but also knowing of the testing and consecration required before the fulfillment of God's promises could be received, he proposed an easier way". As I pondered this statement I realized it's the essence of what I've been writing you about.

To fulfill your purpose you must not take any of the easy and wide roads Satan presents you with but stay on the narrow road tried and tested by Christ himself. I guarantee you will wonder why you have it so hard spiritually when so and so seems to be on easy street maybe even doing what you feel called to do.

To ease your mind I will say so and so may have already been through this consecration process. Many times someone goes through a season of being in the dark and obscure to the world before they are successful. Their success seems like it was overnight but in reality you just never saw Christ being formed in them.

On the other hand it's possible they skipped the process and are successful because they are operating in the natural but following God's Spiritual laws which will work to some degree for anyone. In which case they have taken the wide path and won't be able to sustain what they have because they didn't get it the righteous way.

But really, none of this is good for you to dwell on. They will rise and fall just like you by the hand of God. They are His business and if he hasn't given you the opportunity to know by which path they have gained success- then let it go. Loose jealousy and covetousness from your soul. You cannot hang on to it and see the prosperity of your soul and ministry.

You must know their success does not diminish yours. Their purpose is not yours nor is yours theirs. It's that simple. You just stay on the path God has given you no matter how long it seems you are hidden. Personally, I think the longer you remain hidden the better you are. There is a real threat to your purpose when it becomes seen by others before you are ready. You could get off track by following their idea of the path you should take and not God's.

God is the one who is keeping you in this womb of darkness knowing your seed of faith is growing into something beautiful. He knows how long you need to germinate before you can break through into the sunlight. He knows the tests and the trials you will endure once you – the real you of purpose- is revealed. There will be the intense heat of scrutiny, wind of changing popularity, storms trying to blow you down, and drought. Any of these could kill purpose in you <u>if</u> you sprout <u>before</u> your time. If you let your time of darkness be as fruitful as possible then you will find yourself to be strong even when you feel weak. Through steadfastness of faith you will be able to go on with your Divine mission no matter what circumstances surround you.

When thinking about having our faith tested we can look to the Bible and know through it we're being purified, our character is being developed and we are learning perseverance. An increase in spiritual testing is the intense training needed for your own growth. You learn to defeat spiritual foes by placing less and less confidence in your own self and ability and find living a humble life in Christ is where you are most comfortable and victorious. He is your love and strength and it's with Him that you are seated in Heavenly places or spheres (the word I've come to love!) and by Him you've become a vessel to receive authority.

What an important statement. <u>We have become vessels to receive God's authority</u>. This is why we've been going through the process of tests and trials. This is why we've been seeking Christ with all our hearts. It's not about our own gain now. We've laid down our flesh and idols to live by the Spirit. Through experience we've proven our love for God and have been made ready to serve. By being in readiness or in service to God, I don't mean necessarily through the ministries in existence right now. Many of them have too much earthly design to bring about the Heavenly.

However, I believe all over the world there are men and women who've come to this same spot as we have. The true Church, the Holy Nation of God, which lives in us and is connected together through the Holy Spirit has awakened! He has strengthened us to fight for the freedom of others. We are alive right now to engage and be engaged by the enemy in spiritual battle for something bigger than ourselves.

When I was combatting spiritually in the Chinese hospital for the right to believe in an insane idea- a Living God exists who isn't seen- you don't think it was just for my benefit do you? I have never felt such intense pressure to deny the existence of God before because I've never been in a country where the demonic rulers had so much authority to keep people blinded to Christ.

In China, while the government does allow a certain amount of Bibles to be distributed there are untold millions who have never even heard of Jesus Christ. Letting in a specified amount of Bibles is a freedom the government has allowed in order to say they are not keeping people from learning about Christianity.

Their government is under the influence of demonic rulers who have tried to silence Christianity by only allowing it to grow at a pace they are comfortable with. But they will never be able to keep people from knowing God since the Kingdom is within. While waiting for Bella's release from the doctors, I fought the demonic ruler every Chinese person has to fight if they are to be delivered out of darkness and placed into the Kingdom of Light. I may never physically see the fruit of my stand but I know I will see it one day in Heaven.

Because I put my foot down and planted myself in faith, I had to be willing to defend it. When we got home from China amidst all the chaos and life changing situations which come with a new child, I was determined to find an organization who was getting Bibles into China. I found one right away and in Bella's name I gave financially so someone would be able to read about the God they fought so hard to know. Prayerfully I hope one of those Bibles with Bella's name will get into the hands of her family and in the end they will be able to rejoice in Heaven together and declare: God is good and has turned all the enemy meant for evil into good.

Looking back at the battles all through our adoption and in the dark night of my soul I realized I was fighting for others to be able to resist the enemy through patience, endurance and steadfastness to see God's promises come to pass.

God has designated us (The Church) to teach and by example demonstrate to the heavenly beings the depths of his love, grace, mercy and power. It's up to us to overcome by the power of the Word and the Blood. As you progress toward your purpose in Christ the battles will intensify. The early battles will seem simple enough but the more you keep pressing in the harder they become as you deny Self and self-will in increasing measure.

And so, when thinking of your own life purpose and battlefield:

- ❖ What is it the enemy is pressing your soul to deny or give up? <u>Pay attention and fight for your dream.</u>
- ❖ Are you fighting fears over being called of God to do something you don't think you can? <u>God is with you!</u>
- ❖ Are you being pressed to quit just as victory is imminent? <u>Don't do it!</u>

- ❖ Do you feel like you need to do something to get your purpose going in the direction you want it to? <u>Don't move in your own strength! Only go by and with the Spirit of God.</u>

- ❖ Does the enemy want you to feel alone, isolated and in the dark? <u>Check your thoughts! Then, look up and behold Jesus Christ who is the lifter of your head.</u>

Be patient through the consecration process and make it your aim to not lead yourself out of it but let the perfect work be done. Patience is the entry point into your Promised Land. Resist unbelief and don't allow it to keep you from completing your assignment and walking in the blessing God has assigned to you. Let the Lord be your guide and only walk when and where He leads. Watch as His strength is able to supply you with everything you need just as you need it. Your only need is more of Him.

God has confidence in you and knows you will win by the power of the resurrection of His Son that rests upon you. Just like He believed in Job, He believes in you. He's trained you for a very specific battle and I hope you see it's for this purpose you will stand. You have been given permission to explore some aspect of God which will give you a key to the kingdom.

You'll use your key to conquer in the spiritual realm for the reality of your victory to be brought to earth in some way. Keys open up doors and gates. You will open something – for yourself and others- to walk through and experience an aspect of God's goodness. Others are being trained and supplied for their field of battle. They will gain keys too. Our fields may be different but our battles are the same. We all must overcome the hindrances designed to keep us from doing God's will. What is God's will? Jesus told us, "Thy Kingdom come, Thy Will be done <u>on earth as it is in Heaven</u>"! God's will is for us to bring heaven to earth.

Most importantly God has not left you completely alone for any battle. You have a great promise that Christ will never leave you. He is the Good Shepard and lets us go out and come in –in Him. In Him we have freedom to move about as we need to. He is our husband and we are his bride.

Holy Spirit is our Guide and let us not forget the great company of angels who are here and reserved to help and minister to the heirs of salvation. The angels are given to us to do those things we cannot do for ourselves and to work out situations for our favor. But we must first receive our authority from the Father then command and loose these mighty ones daily for the benefit of ourselves and others. The Bible tells us "we have not because we ask not". When you become one with the Father God through being in Christ, you will begin asking again and having a joy made complete!

God's design and predetermined destiny is for you to win and after the battle you be found standing. I don't mean standing as in barely getting by after just being whipped by an enemy or situation. I mean standing in victory and with victorious life. Joyful for a new day. Once you've become a vessel ready to receive authority you will become joyful to be in command of a regiment of heavenly host. Joy comes from entering into God's plan. Part of this joy is attaining victory. Being victorious. You might be attacked but it will not prosper in your life. Things which were hard before while in the consecration process will become easy. You have now entered into God's rest! Wow!

I feel like I happened upon the Throne Room of God. But I didn't. It wasn't random. The Father is Judge. We have a right to have our day in the courtroom of Heaven when our unseen enemy is harassing us without cause. Whether the demonic was harassing me as a child of God or whether he unlawfully was holding Bella I don't know.

But my concentrated thoughts of Light brought me closer to God. Then I was allowed to be "in the Spirit" and in the place where earthly thoughts could not hinder my mind and knowledge of God. This is the place we need our souls to occupy more and more as it's the place our spirits live in at all times. Seeing into Heaven is possible for every believer and will completely change your outlook on life and eternity.

Now is the time and dispensation of the Spirit and the sons of God to become manifest. We must do our best to usher in as many believers as will have the fortitude to believe in what they cannot understand into the sphere of being "in the Father" so the greater works of Christ will be done.

Freely receive all the armor God supplies. And after you've done all – STAND!

LIGHT FROM A DARK NIGHT

LIGHT FROM A DARK NIGHT

18 Positioned

You have now become a vessel to rule! Hearing from God and commanding the host of Heaven is exhilarating. There is no God like ours. He delights in his children actively taking part in his plans and purposes for the earth through prayer and declaration. In so doing we are filled with great pleasure and fulfilment.

While writing for Letter of Light I received two most beautiful visions which I'd like to share with you. They are both pictures of heaven. I feel they will be helpful for you to understand what you may look like POSTIONED in the spirit realm.

"Vision of the Armies of God" by Anne Grove

Posted on November 3, 2015

"I saw many coming together to form groups or military like companies. Those in the companies formed in groups of three lines. Each company or troupe consisted of three rows of the multitudes.

Coming to the front of each company was a mighty angelic warrior. Each angelic being stood at attention facing God. Coming to stand next to each warrior angel was a mighty son (male and female) of God. The sons of God took hold of the angel's hand and they both faced God with their company standing behind.

Each company received a blessing and power. Suddenly one company at a time received an order from God. They did not debate over their order - they immediately went to battle.

After I saw this scene I heard:

THE HOST IS BEING ASSIGNED AND ALIGNED

GIFTS ARE BEING CONFERRED

TARGETS ARE IDENTIFIED

PLANS ARE DRAWN

BATTLES ARE BEGUN

WAR IS HERE

VICTORY IS DETERMINED

REWARDS ARE WORTHY"

At the time I received this word from God I thought those aligning behind us and the mighty warrior angel were people- members of the Body of Christ. Now I understand they are members of the Heavenly Host. The Heavenly Host move quickly and without reserve when commanded and sent. Humans wouldn't move so readily. We may stop to think about whether the command makes sense or not.

As a vessel fit to rule you have been assigned a mighty warring angel and a company of heavenly host. This is why you are filled with so much joy! You are able to affect so much in the earth. You have power to aid and help wherever you decide to send the host in your command. I urge you to seek out those prophets in the earth right now with revelation into this very special plan and purpose of God for his sons and daughters. One such prophet is Kat Kerr. I recommend reading her books and everything she has spoken.

Notice God has aligned and assigned the Host. I believe they are thrilled to partner with sons and daughters of God. The whole earth is groaning, waiting, desiring for the sons and daughters of God to manifest bringing with them every form of restoration.

God has given each company gifts and specific targets. Remember each one of us has specific gifts and assignments. You have the right gifts for your assignment. So important not to covet another's gift or assignment! They are not yours and you don't want yours left on the table unfulfilled!

God has plans and they have been drawn. We must seek him for the wisdom of His plans and designs. We must be intentional about what we are doing. Have strategy - seek God's strategy.

The battles have already begun. Some of these battles we will fight are ancient in nature. War is here. It's an all-out assault and I don't mean against us. We are on the offense all over the world. We are not using physical weapons but spiritual ones. How exciting is this time!

And VICTORY is determined. We have the confidence of being assigned as victorious before we ever begin. We can't lose by staying on the path God has assigned us.

Think of the greatest reward you could ever be given and know God will make your ideas look too small. What could be given to a victorious warrior of the MOST HIGH GOD? Whatever "it" is we know one thing: It is WORTHY and we will spend an eternity enjoying it.

The next vision was given to me and posted on March 3, 2015

The New Covenant and the Sea of Mercy by Anne Grove
"Many times I'm given visuals to compliment my prayers and yesterday was one of those special moments. I was

concentrating on the blood of Christ and his sacrifice for our sins when a vision opened up.

I saw myself sitting down on a stone bench. I was in an arena of sorts with a great multitude which was gathered together. The stone bench was at the back of the arena so I could see all who were already in their seats. They were not sitting so I guess they were in their designated places.

I was clothed in armor or what seemed to be battle clothing. A man came forth to wash my feet. I knew him to be my Lord Jesus. He spoke nothing to me but lovingly washed my feet. When he was done I stood up and noticed my clothing had been changed from battle clothes to royal robes. I wore a long red robe and a crown was upon my head.

I took the arm of my Savior and He escorted me down an aisle. At the end of the aisle was the spectacularly lit Throne of God. It was all light which shone from above. I knelt and placed my crown before the Throne. There were so many crowns laid down before God it was beautiful. I went and took my place.

Jesus began to speak to the Father who sat on the throne. There was no sound being made by anyone else but Jesus. He spoke of the sin of the world. He spoke of our sin. He recounted the sacrifice he made for all mankind. As He was speaking, my heart wept knowing I did not deserve such love. I did not deserve this sacrifice on my behalf. I bent down as I wept.

I was moved to look up and saw not only myself bowed down to Him but all were. Everyone, thousands upon thousands knew we did not deserve what He had done for us. Jesus kept speaking of His Blood, of the sacrifice which was the NEW COVENANT.

Suddenly I saw the multitude as a whole. Bent down all that was seen was the red from our robes. Before the Throne of God was what looked like a sea of red. A sea of blood. A sea of sacrifice. All the Father could see was this Sea.

The Sea spoke and said, "Mercy". The vision ended.

Hebrews 12:22-24 (AMP)

22 But you have come to Mount Zion and to the city of the living God, the heavenly Jerusalem, and to myriads of angels [in festive gathering],23 and to the general assembly and assembly of the firstborn who are registered [as citizens] in heaven, and to God, who is Judge of all, and to the spirits of the righteous (the redeemed in heaven) who have been made perfect [bringing them to their final glory], 24 and to Jesus, the Mediator of a new covenant [uniting God and man], and to the sprinkled blood, which speaks [of mercy], a better and nobler and more gracious message than the blood of Abel [which cried out for vengeance].

This is what I saw- the general assembly! The New Covenant Jesus Christ wants us to remember is MERCY. The law of mercy is higher than vengeance. Mercy triumphed and completely covered over each and every believer.

If you ever feel unworthy of the sacrifice Jesus made for you- it's true and in humility its right to acknowledge it. But he died to cover our life with forgiveness of sins and mercy. And

He gave us Communion- a common union with each other. When we drink from the Cup, we join with each other to participate in His Blood. Whether we know it or not we are the Sea of Mercy and are on the earth right now. When taking communion today- let's focus on praying Mercy for all who need it and will receive it."

In this vision the Lord showed me many things. As it pertains to being POSITIONED in Him, I want you to pay very close attention to Hebrews 12. The first part of the verse is speaking about angels and those with citizenship in heaven. Then the writer also includes the spirits of the redeemed. They are two different classes of people. Those alive who have citizenship in heaven and those who have gone home already. If you are alive in Christ right now, then you belong to the first group. You are part of this heavenly assembly right NOW!

In the first part of the vision I wore battle clothes. Then Jesus refreshed and washed me clean. Remember the night Jesus was betrayed he washed the disciple's feet? Peter was indignant and felt the Lord should not wash his feet. But Jesus said those who aren't washed have no part "in him".

Just in case some who read this book think the mighty sons and daughters of God are undeserving of our position I'll fill you in on something right now. We are completely undeserving <u>and we know it better than anyone</u> – even you!

But what we don't deserve God has given freely- Mercy and Grace. All we did was receive it.

We're not special. We're not unique. We are however dearly beloved of Father God because we are obedient to Christ and love him. God loves us because we love and trust his Son. Because of this relationship we've been made alive in our spirit and led by God through the fire of tests and trials so our hearts would be pure by the time we reached this destination of ruling and commanding heavenly host.

Many followers of God have desired fire to come down from heaven to destroy their personal enemies. But through the process of sanctification we now love our enemies and realize the fight is not with human foes but spiritual. We take our fight inward to the denial of self and upward to the destruction of demonic rulers of wickedness.

You wear two garments: a warrior's garment and royal robes washed clean by Jesus. Right now you are in battle and must wear and put on the armor God supplies. But when joining the Assembly of God your battle clothes are changed to royal robes.

It's only fitting as we wear these royal robes of pure light we understand the key we've been given. In humility we bow low before Jesus in the Sea of Mercy; possessing deep knowledge of our personal sin and the remarkable, undeniable gift we have been given. By His precious blood we've been made completely clean and whole through the binding sacrifice he made once for all. To Him be Glory and Honor forever and ever! Amen.

LIGHT FROM A DARK NIGHT

About the Author

Anne M Grove is wife, mother, author and blogger. Her passion is to encourage, strengthen and equip women through God's word so they can walk in their divine purpose.

For more information and further reading visit:

www.letteroflight.com

www.annemgrove.com

Connect with Anne:

Facebook: Letter of Light Ministries

[i] 2 Corinthians 1:3-4 underline mine

[ii] Ephesians 2:10

[iii] Anne and Rob Grove were in China November 6-21, 2013 to adopt a child.

[iv] 1 Thessalonians 3:1-5

[v] 1 Thessalonians 2:4

[vi] 1 Corinthians 4:2

[vii] 2Peter 3:18

[viii] Romans 5:1-5

[ix] Romans 8:29-31

[x] Ephesians 6:12

[xi] Ephesians 3:10

[xii] 2 Corinthians 10:4

[xiii] Ephesians 6:14

[xiv] Romans 8:28

[xv] 1 Peter 1:9

[xvi] 1 Corinthians 7:14

[xvii] Isaiah 66:9

[xviii] Hebrews 12:2

[xix] 2 Corinthians 11:30

[xx] 2 Corinthians 12:10

[xxi] 2Peter 2:9

[xxii] 1 John 2:16 (author underline)

[xxiii] 2 Corinthians 12:9

[xxiv] 1 Corinthians 13:7

[xxv] Galatians 5: 22-23

[xxvi] James 1:2-4 THE MESSAGE

[xxvii] Hebrews 6:12

[xxviii] Hebrews 4:12

[xxix] Romans 8:35-39

[xxx] Daniel 10:12

[xxxi] Daniel 10:12

[xxxii] John 14:17

[xxxiii] John 7:38

[xxxiv] Colossians 1:27

[xxxv] John 3:6 (AMPC- Amplified Bible Classic Edition)

[xxxvi] 1 Corinthians 14:2 (AMPC) underlines mine

[xxxvii] 1 Corinthians 13:8-12

[xxxviii] Praying Medic blog post

[xxxix] G1100 Strong's Exhaustive Concordance of the Bible Updated 2007

[xl] 1 Corinthians 1:10 (AMPC)

[xli] John 13:35

[xlii] John 14:6

[xliii] John 14:21

[xliv] John 3:3

[xlv] 1 John 4:1

[xlvi] 1 Thessalonians 5:20-21

[xlvii] John 17:24

[xlviii] Matthew 11:28

[xlix] Matthew 11:28 Matthew Henry Biblical Commentary kindle location 207774

[l] Colossians 3:2

[li] G1718 Strong's Exhaustive Concordance of the Bible Updated 2007

[lii] Romans 7:18 (AMPC)

[liii] G1785 Strong's Exhaustive Concordance of the Bible 2007

[liv] G5083 and G2334 Strong's Concordance of the Bible 2007

[lv] Dave Roberson www.daveroberson.org

[lvi] Charles G. Finney "How to Experience the Higher Life"

[lvii] Daniel 10: 11-14 (AMPC)

[lviii] Ephesians 4:1-2

[lix] Malachi 3:2-4

[lx] Malachi 3:5 (AMPC)

[lxi] 2 Peter 2:9-10

[lxii] Online dictionary

[lxiii] Ephesians 2:1-4

Made in the USA
Middletown, DE
10 May 2018